COMPREHENSIVE RESEARCH
AND STUDY GUIDE

BLOOM'S
MAJOR
DRAMATISTS

Shakespeare's
Histories

EDITED AND WITH AN
INTRODUCTION BY HAROLD BLOOM

BLOOM'S MAJOR DRAMATISTS

Anton Chekhov
Henrik Ibsen
Arthur Miller
Eugene O'Neill
Shakespeare's Comedies
Shakespeare's Histories
Shakespeare's Romances
Shakespeare's Tragedies
George Bernard Shaw
Tennessee Williams

BLOOM'S MAJOR NOVELISTS

Jane Austen
The Brontës
Willa Cather
Charles Dickens
William Faulkner
F. Scott Fitzgerald
Nathaniel Hawthorne
Ernest Hemingway
Toni Morrison
John Steinbeck
Mark Twain
Alice Walker

BLOOM'S MAJOR SHORT STORY WRITERS

William Faulkner
F. Scott Fitzgerald
Ernest Hemingway
O. Henry
James Joyce
Herman Melville
Flannery O'Connor
Edgar Allan Poe
J. D. Salinger
John Steinbeck
Mark Twain
Eudora Welty

BLOOM'S MAJOR WORLD POETS

Geoffrey Chaucer
Emily Dickinson
John Donne
T. S. Eliot
Robert Frost
Langston Hughes
John Milton
Edgar Allan Poe
Shakespeare's Poems & Sonnets
Alfred, Lord Tennyson
Walt Whitman
William Wordsworth

BLOOM'S NOTES

The Adventures of Huckleberry Finn
Aeneid
The Age of Innocence
Animal Farm
The Autobiography of Malcolm X
The Awakening
Beloved
Beowulf
Billy Budd, Benito Cereno, & Bartleby the Scrivener
Brave New World
The Catcher in the Rye
Crime and Punishment
The Crucible

Death of a Salesman
A Farewell to Arms
Frankenstein
The Grapes of Wrath
Great Expectations
The Great Gatsby
Gulliver's Travels
Hamlet
Heart of Darkness & The Secret Sharer
Henry IV, Part One
I Know Why the Caged Bird Sings
Iliad
Inferno
Invisible Man
Jane Eyre
Julius Caesar

King Lear
Lord of the Flies
Macbeth
A Midsummer Night's Dream
Moby-Dick
Native Son
Nineteen Eighty-Four
Odyssey
Oedipus Plays
Of Mice and Men
The Old Man and the Sea
Othello
Paradise Lost
A Portrait of the Artist as a Young Man
The Portrait of a Lady

Pride and Prejudice
The Red Badge of Courage
Romeo and Juliet
The Scarlet Letter
Silas Marner
The Sound and the Fury
The Sun Also Rises
A Tale of Two Cities
Tess of the D'Urbervilles
Their Eyes Were Watching God
To Kill a Mockingbird
Uncle Tom's Cabin
Wuthering Heights

COMPREHENSIVE RESEARCH
AND STUDY GUIDE

BLOOM'S
MAJOR
DRAMATISTS

Shakespeare's
Histories

EDITED AND WITH AN INTRODUCTION
BY HAROLD BLOOM

First Printing
1 3 5 7 9 8 6 4 2

Library of Congress Cataloging-in-Publication Data
Shakespeare's histories / edited and with an introduction by Harold Bloom.
    p.   cm. — (Bloom's major dramatists : comprehensive research and study guide)
Includes bibliographical references and index.
ISBN 0-7910-5241-9
1. Shakespeare, William, 1564–1616—Histories—Examinations
Study guides.   2. Historical drama, English—Examinations Study guides.
I. Bloom, Harold.   II. Series.
PR2982.S49   2000
822.3'3 — dc21   99-36774
                                                               CIP

Chelsea House Publishers
1974 Sproul Road, Suite 400
Broomall, PA 19008-0914

The Chelsea House world wide web
address is www.chelseahouse.com

Contributing Editor: Tenley Williams

Contents

User's Guide

This volume is designed to present biographical, critical, and bibliographical information on the author's best-known or most important works. Following Harold Bloom's editor's note and introduction is a detailed biography of the author, discussing major life events and important literary accomplishments. A plot summary of each play follows, tracing significant themes, patterns, and motifs in the work.

A selection of critical extracts, derived from previously published material from leading critics, analyzes aspects of each play. The extracts consist of statements from the author, if available, early reviews of the work, and later evaluations up to the present. A bibliography of the author's writings (including a complete list of all works written, cowritten, edited, and translated), a list of additional books and articles on the author and his or her work, and an index of themes and ideas in the author's writings conclude the volume.

~

Harold Bloom is Sterling Professor of the Humanities at Yale University and Henry W. and Albert A. Berg Professor of English at the New York University Graduate School. He is the author of over 20 books and the editor of more than 30 anthologies of literary criticism.

Professor Bloom's works include *Shelley's Mythmaking* (1959), *The Visionary Company* (1961), *Blake's Apocalypse* (1963), *Yeats* (1970), *A Map of Misreading* (1975), *Kabbalah and Criticism* (1975), and *Agon: Toward a Theory of Revisionism* (1982). *The Anxiety of Influence* (1973) sets forth Professor Bloom's provocative theory of the literary relationships between the great writers and their predecessors. His most recent books include *The American Religion* (1992), *The Western Canon* (1994), *Omens of Millennium: The Gnosis of Angels, Dreams, and Resurrection* (1996), and *Shakespeare: The Invention of the Human* (1998), a finalist for the 1998 National Book Award.

Professor Bloom earned his Ph.D. from Yale University in 1955 and has served on the Yale faculty since then. He is a 1985 MacArthur Foundation Award recipient, served as the Charles Eliot Norton Professor of Poetry at Harvard University in 1987–88, and has received honorary degrees from the universities of Rome and Bologna. In 1999, Professor Bloom received the prestigious American Academy of Arts and Letters Gold Medal for Criticism.

Currently, Harold Bloom is the editor of numerous Chelsea House volumes of literary criticism, including the series BLOOM'S NOTES, BLOOM'S MAJOR SHORT STORY WRITERS, BLOOM'S MAJOR POETS, MAJOR LITERARY CHARACTERS, MODERN CRITICAL VIEWS, MODERN CRITICAL INTERPRETATIONS, and WOMEN WRITERS OF ENGLISH AND THEIR WORKS.

Editor's Note

My Introduction centers upon the sublime Sir John Falstaff, the glory of Shakespeare's history-plays.

Critical Views of *Richard III* include A. W. Schlegel, while *Henry IV, Part 1* is illuminated by Robert N. Watson and Paul M. Cubeta, among others. *Henry IV, Part 2* has comments by Sigurd Burckhardt that are particularly useful.

Henry V receives a full range of critical reactions from Schlegel and Dr. Samuel Johnson on to their devoted follower, myself.

Introduction

HAROLD BLOOM

Shakespeare's greatest history play is the ten-act drama constituted by *King Henry IV – Parts 1 and 2*. Judged as a single work, this vast Falstaffiad is one of Shakespeare's major achievements, akin to *Antony and Cleopatra, As You Like It, Twelfth Night, Measure for Measure,* and *The Winter's Tale.* The four high tragedies—*Hamlet, Othello, King Lear,* and *Macbeth*—stand a little apart, in their own cosmos, as does *The Tempest.* The Falstaffiad is at the center of Shakespeare's work, and its superb protagonist, Sir John Falstaff, rivals Shakespeare's other triumphs in the invention of the human: Hamlet, Rosalind, Iago, Lear, Macbeth, Cleopatra.

Criticism, particularly in our century, is frequently both inaccurate and unkind about Falstaff. That is because the brilliant and uncanny wit outfaces and outrages his undertakers. He also buries them. Falstaff is so large a form of life and thought that all of us have trouble catching up with him. He confounds our expectations, and calls our compromises into question.

Falstaff's vitality, his battle-cry being "Give me life," is the most crucial of his attributes, but his intelligence is endless and matches his exuberance. Nearly everything he says rewards much pondering, for he beholds reality, and not the shams that mock it. Sir John long since has seen through the "honor" for which Hotspur and Prince Hal compete. Falstaff may be an outrageous Socrates, but so was Socrates. Sir John's other affinities are with Cervantes's Sancho Panza and with Rabelais's Panurge, and most closely with Chaucer's Wife of Bath. Heroic vitalists all, these abide as images of gusto in its highest form, allied to wisdom and to laughter.

Aligned against Falstaff are the state and time, and the state, in the guise of the newly crowned Henry V, will destroy him. Though legions of scholars have acclaimed this destruction, their sentiments are not Shakespeare's. Shakespeare carefully excluded Falstaff from *Henry V,* except for Mistress Quickly's poignant description of Sir John's deathbed scene. Can we imagine King Henry V eloquently saluting his "happy few" if Falstaff were among them, bottle of sack in his holster?

In his darker moments, Falstaff is haunted by the parable of Lazarus the leper and a purple-clad glutton who refuses him food and water (Luke 16: 19–26). This is a parable of rejection, first of Lazarus by the wealthy glutton, and then of the glutton by Abraham, who takes Lazarus into his bosom while refusing to aid the stingy rich man, who burns in hell. Falstaff's three allusions to this parable reveal his own fear of rejection by Hal, an apprehension that is realized when Falstaff kneels to the purple-clad, newly crowned Henry V, and is denounced and exiled. Shakespeare's answer comes in Mistress Quickly's declaration that the deceased Falstaff is "in Arthur's bosom," a clear displacement of Abraham's bosom.

A. C. Bradley, nearly a century ago, made the definitive comment upon the sublime Falstaff:

> And, therefore, we praise him, we laud him, for he offends none but the virtuous, and denies that life is real or life is earnest, and delivers us from the apprehension of such nightmares, and lifts us into the atmosphere of perfect freedom. ❀

Biography of
William Shakespeare

William Shakespeare was born in Stratford-on-Avon in April 1564 into a family of some prominence. His father, John Shakespeare, was a glover and merchant of leather goods, who earned enough to marry the daughter of his father's landlord, Mary Arden, in 1557. John Shakespeare was a prominent citizen in Stratford, and at one point, he served as an alderman and bailiff.

Shakespeare presumably attended the Stratford grammar school, where he would have received an education in Latin, but he did not go on to either Oxford or Cambridge Universities. Little is recorded about Shakespeare's early life; indeed, the first record of his life after his christening is of his marriage to Anne Hathaway in 1582 in the church at Temple Grafton, near Stratford. He would have been required to obtain a special license from the bishop as security that there was no impediment to the marriage. Peter Alexander states in his book *Shakespeare's Life and Art* that marriage at this time in England required neither a church nor a priest or, for that matter, even a document—only a declaration of the contracting parties in the presence of witnesses. Thus, it was customary, though not mandatory, to follow the marriage with a church ceremony.

Little is known about William and Anne Shakespeare's marriage. Their first child, Susanna, was born in May 1583, and twins, Hamnet and Judith Shakespeare, followed in 1585. Later on, Susanna married Dr. John Hall, but the younger daughter, Judith, remained unmarried. When Hamnet died in Stratford in 1596, the boy was only eleven years old.

We have no record of Shakespeare's activities for the seven years after the birth of his twins, but by 1592 he was in London working as an actor. He was also apparently well-known as a playwright, for reference is made of him by his contemporary Robert Greene in *A Groatsworth of Wit* as "an upstart crow."

Several companies of actors were in London at this time. Shakespeare may have had connection with one or more of them before 1592, but we have no record that tells us definitely. However, we do know of his long association with the most famous and successful troupe, the Lord Chamberlain's Men. (When James I came to the throne in 1603, after Elizabeth's death, the troupe's name changed to the King's Men.) In 1599 the Lord Chamberlain's Men provided the financial backing for the construction of their own theater, the Globe.

The Globe was begun by a carpenter named James Burbage and finished by his two sons, Cuthbert and Robert. To escape the jurisdiction of the Corporation of London, which was composed of conservative Puritans who opposed the theatre's "licentiousness," James Burbage built the Globe just outside London, in the Liberty of Holywell beside Finsbury Fields. This also meant that the Globe was safer from the threats that lurked in London's crowded streets, like plague and other diseases, as well as rioting mobs. When James Burbage died in 1598, his sons completed the Globe's construction. Shakespeare played a vital role, financially and otherwise, in the construction of the theater, which was finally occupied some time before May 16, 1599.

Shakespeare not only acted with the Globe's company of actors; he was also a shareholder and eventually became the troupe's most important playwright. The company included London's most famous actors, who inspired the creation of Shakespeare's well-known characters such as Hamlet and Lear, as well as his clowns and fools.

In his early years, however, Shakespeare did not confine himself to the theater. He also composed some mythological-erotic poetry, such as *Venus and Adonis* and *The Rape of Lucrece,* both of which were dedicated to the earl of Southampton. Shakespeare was successful enough that in 1597 he was able to purchase his own home in Stratford, New Place. He could even call himself a gentleman, for his father had been granted a coat of arms.

By 1598 Shakespeare had written some of his most famous works, *Romeo and Juliet, The Comedy of Errors, A Midsummer Night's Dream, The Merchant of Venice, Two Gentleman of Verona,* and *Love's Labour's Lost,* as well as his historical plays *Henry VI, Parts 1–3, Richard II, Richard III, Henry IV, Parts 1 and 2,* and *King John.* Somewhere around the turn of the century, Shakespeare wrote his romantic comedies *As You Like It, Twelfth Night,* and *Much Ado About Nothing,* as well as *Henry V,* the last of his history plays in the Prince Hal series. During the next ten years he wrote his great tragedies, *Hamlet, Macbeth, Othello, King Lear,* and *Antony and Cleopatra.*

At this time, the theater was burgeoning in London; the public took an avid interest in drama, the audiences were large, the plays demonstrated an enormous range of variety, and playwrights competed for approval. By 1613, however, the rising tide of Puritanism had changed the theater. With the desertion of the theaters by the middle classes, the acting companies were compelled to depend more on the aristocracy, which also meant that they now had to cater to a more sophisticated audience.

Perhaps this change in London's artistic atmosphere contributed to Shakespeare's reasons for leaving London after 1612. His retirement from the theater is sometimes thought to be evidence that his artistic skills were waning. During this time, however, he wrote *The Tempest* and *Henry VIII.* He also wrote the "tragicomedies," *Pericles, Cymbeline,* and *The Winter's Tale.* These were thought to be inspired by Shakespeare's personal problems, and have sometimes been considered proof of his greatly diminished abilities.

However, so far as biographical facts indicate, the circumstances of his life at this time do not imply any personal problems. He was in good health, financially secure, and enjoyed an excellent reputation. Indeed, although he was settled in Stratford at this time, he made frequent visits to London, enjoying and participating in events at the royal court, directing rehearsals, and attending to other business matters.

In addition to his brilliant and enormous contributions to the theater, Shakespeare remained a poetic genius throughout the years, publishing a renowned and critically acclaimed sonnet cycle in 1609. Shakespeare's contribution to this popular poetic genre is all the more amazing in his break with contemporary notions of subject matter. Shakespeare idealized the beauty of man as an object of praise and devotion (rather than the Petrarchan tradition of the idealized, unattainable woman). In the same spirit of breaking with tradition, Shakespeare also treated themes which hitherto had been considered off limits—the dark, sexual side of a woman as opposed to the Petrarchan ideal of a chaste and remote love object. He also expanded the sonnet's emotional range, including such emotions as delight, pride, shame, disgust, sadness, and fear.

When Shakespeare died in 1616, no collected edition of his works had ever been published, although some of his plays had been printed in separate unauthorized editions. (Some of these were taken from his manuscripts, some from the actors' prompt books, and others were reconstructed from memory by actors or spectators.) In 1623, two members of the King's Men, John Hemings and Henry Condell, published a collection of all the plays they considered to be authentic, the First Folio.

Included in the First Folio is a poem by Shakespeare's contemporary Ben Jonson, an outstanding playwright and critic in his own right. Jonson paid tribute to Shakespeare's genius, proclaiming his superiority to what previously had been held as the models for literary excellence—the Greek and Latin writers. "Triumph, my Britain, thou hast one to show / To whom all scenes of Europe homage owe. / He was not of an age, but for all time!"

Jonson was the first to state what has been said so many times since. Having captured what is permanent and universal to all human beings at all times, Shakespeare's genius continues to inspire us, and the critical debate about his works never ceases. ❀

Plot Summary of
Richard III

In this play Shakespeare explores the power and the limitations of evil. Richard III is a complex figure, both charming and coarse, sometimes brutal. His lust for power is the foundation of tragedy; his hubris ensures that he is the agent of his own destruction. Retribution is the response to his evil actions and the form of his downfall.

The play opens with the arrival of Richard, duke of Gloucester, in London. His brother King Edward IV is slowly dying, and Richard is intent upon securing the crown for himself (**Act I**, scene 1). In his opening soliloquy he describes his shape that marks him as "Deform'd, unfinish'd, . . . / And that so lamely and unfashionable / That dogs bark at me as I halt by them." He discloses his motives and predicts the action of the play: "[S]ince I cannot prove a lover, / . . . I am determined to prove a villain, / . . . . Plots have I laid, . . . / To set my brother Clarence and the king / In deadly hate to one against the other; / And if King Edward be as true and just / As I am subtle, false, and treacherous, / This day should Clarence closely be mew'd up [caged, like a hawk], / About a prophecy, which says that G / Of Edward's heirs the murderer shall be." Richard convinces the king that "G" is George, duke of Clarence, and the king has him committed to the Tower of London. Richard then convinces Lord Hastings, who has just been released from prison himself, that those who were Hastings's enemies are also responsible for Clarence's imprisonment.

In scene 2 King Henry VI has died and Richard approaches the mourning Lady Anne (Neville), an heiress and widow of the son of the late king, with a proposal of marriage. She knows that Richard was responsible for the deaths of both her husband and her father-in-law. In this scene Richard annihilates moral order as he shows his rhetorical skills by convincing her to marry him. He offers her his sword with which to execute him herself, saying to her "Nay, do not pause: for I did kill King Henry, / But 'twas thy beauty that provoked me. / Nay, now dispatch; t'was I that stabb'd young Edward, / But 'twas thy heavenly face that set me on. / Take up the sword again, or take up me." Anne replies, "Arise, dissembler: though I wish thy death, / I will not be thy executioner." He leaves her, satisfied that she finds him "a marvellous proper man," marvelling himself that he has manipulated her by "the plain devil and dissembling looks." He means to keep her only as long as he needs her to consolidate his power.

Edward IV's wife, Queen Elizabeth, is troubled that Richard has been named Protector of the Realm and guardian of Edward, her young son and heir to the throne (scene 3). The Queen tells Richard that King Edward wants to speak with her and the nobles "of his own royal disposition / And not provoked by any suitor else; / Aiming, belike, at your interior hatred, / Which in your outward action shows itself / Against my kindred, brothers, and myself, / Makes him to send; that thereby he may gather / The ground of your ill-will, and to remove it." On the way to this meeting old Queen Margaret interrupts them. She reminds them of old horrors and, like a "prophetess," predicts new ones for the country and for her family. She warns Lord Buckingham to "take heed of yonder dog [Richard]! / Look, when he fawns, he bites; and when he bites, / His venom tooth will rankle to the death: / Have not to do with him, beware of him; / Sin, death, and hell have set their marks on him, / And all their ministers attend on him." Later she warns, "O, but remember this another day, / When he shall split thy very heart with sorrow, / And say poor Margaret was a prophetess. / Live each of you the subjects to his hate, / And he to yours, and all of you to God's!"

Clarence is murdered in scene 4. Soon after, King Edward dies (**Act II**, scene 2), and Richard conspires with the Duke of Buckingham to succeed Clarence. They must bring young Edward, the Prince of Wales, to London for his coronation. While they are gone, Queen Elizabeth discovers that Richard has imprisoned her brother, Lord Rivers, and another son, Lord Grey, by a previous marriage (scene 4). She laments, "Ay, me, I see the downfall of my house! / The tiger [Richard] now hath seized the gentle hind; / Insulting tyranny begins to jet / Upon the innocent and aweless throne. / Welcome, destruction, death, and massacre! / I see, as in a map, the end of all."

When the Prince of Wales arrives in London, he and his younger brother, the Duke of York, are imprisoned in the Tower of London, supposedly for their safety (**Act III**, scene 1). Sir William Catesby questions Lord Hastings, on Richard's behalf, about the possibility of Richard's succession to the throne. Hastings's refusal to support Richard's claim to the throne ensures that he will die. In scene 3 Rivers, Grey, and Vaughan are beheaded. Before his execution Grey remarks to Rivers, "Now Margaret's curse is fall'n upon our heads, / When she exclaim'd on Hastings, you, and I, / For standing by when Richard stabb'd her son."

Richard calls a meeting of the Council at which he accuses Hastings of treason and condemns him to death (scene 4). Hastings concludes, "O bloody Richard! Miserable England! / I prophesy the fearfull'st time to thee / That ever wretched age hath look'd upon. / Come, lead me to the block; bear him my head. / They smile at me who shortly shall be dead." Buckingham makes a public speech praising Richard and suggesting that the late King Edward's children are illegitimate. The crowd does not believe the slander, nor do they believe that the executions were just (scene 5). However, the city officials do believe that only Richard can quell the civil disorder that seems about to erupt. They plead with Richard to accept the crown; he feigns reluctance, but eventually accepts (scene 7). Richard ascends the throne (**Act IV**, scene 2) and must consolidate his power to ensure it. He first moves to eliminate the legal heirs to the throne, the young princes in the Tower. When Buckingham refuses to arrange the murder, Richard does so himself. Richard also reveals that he will eliminate his wife, Queen Anne, so that he may marry his brother's daughter [the daughter of Edward IV and Queen Elizabeth], "Or else my kingdom stands on brittle glass. / Murder her brothers, and then marry her! / Uncertain way of gain! But I am in / So far in blood that sin will pluck on sin. / Tear-falling pity dwells not in this eye."

The children, the boys, are murdered (scene 3), and Richard's problems multiply. Buckingham, having fled England after falling into disfavor, has raised an army to march against Richard. From France, there is information that the Lancastrian heir, Henry, earl of Richmond, is preparing to move against him (scene 4). Richard must respond to these crises; he must fight them. First, however, he must win the support of Queen Elizabeth in his plan to marry her daughter: "Be opposite all planets of good luck / To my proceedings, if, with pure heart's love, / Immaculate devotion, holy thoughts, / I tender not thy beauteous princely daughter!" She responds, "But thou didst kill my children." He replies, "But in your daughter's womb I bury them: / Where in that nest of spicery they shall breed / Selves of themselves, to your recomforture." His formidable rhetoric wears the woman down and she seems to approve the marriage.

The forces against Richard continue to build, but Buckingham is defeated, captured, and executed (**Act V**, scene 1). Henry, earl of Richmond, lands in England and prepares to engage Richard and his forces at Bosworth Field (scene 2). The night before the battle (scene 3), the ghosts of Richard's victims appear in the dreams of both Richard and Richmond. To Richard these ghosts predict doom; to Richmond, triumph. Although his troops outnumber Richmond's three to one, desertions among his allies trouble Richard further, but he is determined to keep his crown and kingdom. Before the battle, both leaders exhort their troops to fight bravely.

Richard himself is a brave fighter. In scene 4, on foot after his horse is slain, he famously cries, "I have set my life upon a cast, / And I will stand the hazard of the die. / I think there be six Richmonds in the field; / Five have I slain to-day in stead of him. / A horse! a horse! my kingdom for a horse!" In scene 5, Richmond slays Richard and declares an amnesty to all, alive and dead, on both sides: "Inter their bodies as become their births: / Proclaim a pardon to the soldiers fled, / That in submission will return to us: / And then, as we have ta'en the sacrament, / We will unite the white rose and the red. / . . . O, now let Richmond and Elizabeth, / The true succeeders of each royal house, / By God's fair ordinance conjoin together! / . . . Now civil wounds are stopp'd, peace lives again: / That she may long live here, God say amen!" ❀

List of Characters in
Richard III

Richard, duke of Gloucester (later, **Richard III**) was the last English king to die in battle. Shakespeare drew his character from historical accounts of Richard's rise to power during the 15th-century Wars of the Roses found in the works of Edward Hall, Raphael Holinshed, and Sir Thomas More. The negative view of the historical Richard has been much disputed, but Shakespeare was clearly more interested in the character's dramatic possibilities. What makes Richard interesting in the play is the tension between fate and free will that his character embodies. He is both a victim of circumstances and in charge of his own destiny. But, although the play is titled *The Tragedy of Richard III*, his fall is not from greatness, which tragedy requires, but a punishment well-deserved. He is not a good man, but a Machiavel who makes evil his good. He dies in a brave confrontation with Richmond, and although the triumph of good is satisfying, our capacity to respond to and ultimately recoil from Richard's depravity makes him by far the more interesting element.

Queen Margaret is the widow of Henry VI, the Lancastrian ruler overthrown by the York family. Shakespeare's treatment of her character is historically inaccurate, but she proves useful here as a prophet, a knower of family secrets, and a conduit of historical information in portraying Richard's quest for power. An exile who has remained at court, she was once a powerful adversary to Richard, but now she is a shadowy figure, given to visions and curses and predictions of doom. She is Richard's Nemesis (in Greek mythology, the goddess of retribution).

The **Duke of Buckingham** ignores Margaret's warning that Richard's evil nature and the curse she has prophesied will doom all who serve him. Foolish and greedy, Buckingham is manipulated by Richard through flattery, position, and promises of wealth. He finally balks when called upon to have the young princes murdered. When Richard spurns him, he is shocked but attempts to raise an army against him. Captured by Richard, on his way to execution, he recalls Margaret's prophecy.

Queen Elizabeth is the wife of Edward IV. She is a powerful political force, but here she has been weakened by her husband's illness and the danger she is in from Richard. She knows that Richard is to be feared, but she cannot raise an army against him. She is a strong character who never becomes one of Richard's victims. When Richard works to convince her that her daughter should accept him in marriage, her answer is ambiguous. She appears to be won over on her daughter's behalf, but, as we see, the final victory is hers.

Lady Anne Neville is the daughter of the Duke of Warwick and the widow of Henry VI's son, the former Prince of Wales. The contest between Anne and Richard is one of Shakespeare's most powerful scenes. That it occurs early in the play warns us of Richard's uncanny skill in recognizing and exploiting weaknesses in others. He is undeterred by Anne's well-deserved hatred for him and, shockingly, wins her to his bed.

Henry Tudor, earl of Richmond is the grandfather of Shakespeare's own monarch, Queen Elizabeth I, and thus emerges as the champion and peacemaker in the play. He is introduced toward the end of the play, his noble character in direct contrast to Richard's.

George, duke of Clarence is the brother of Richard and Edward IV. He, like Anne, is one of Richard's first victims and a sign of the cycle of cruelty that runs through all Richard's relationships. His trust in his brother is his downfall. Although he is guilty of crimes in his own right, he is never allowed to struggle with his brother for his life, only in his dreams before he is assassinated by Richard's men. His death marks the play's cycle of prophecy and Nemesis – the prediction of doom.

King Edward IV is Richard's brother. An incompetent and gullible monarch, Edward deserves Richard's low opinion, although Shakespeare never suggests that this justifies any of Richard's actions. The character of Edward does suggest that the lack of choice between these two unfit rulers legitimizes the claims of the ideal ruler, Richmond, at the play's end.

Duchess of York is the mother of two kings, Edward IV and Richard III, and their brother, the Duke of Clarence. We learn a great deal about her children through the statements she makes. She never gives Richard her blessing or approval and denounces him at the earliest opportunity. Richard knows the political danger of suggesting that she is an adulteress in order to establish the illegitimacy of Edward IV's sons.

Lord Hastings, the Lord Chamberlain, is a typical Shakespearean gull, a predictable fool. His naive and trusting appearance masks a lust for revenge that leads to his downfall. He is another of Richard's victims, first drawn to power and flattery, then destroyed.

The Prince of Wales and **the Duke of York** are sons of Edward IV. Most striking is their vulnerability to Richard's cruelty without the protection of their maternal uncles. Wales teases his Uncle Richard with fantasies of foreign conquest; York enjoys word games with the uncle who will destroy him. The detailed description of the moments before the boys are murdered is the more intriguing because the mystery of their deaths has never been solved. It remains the most damning element in the case against the historical Richard. ❀

Critical Views on
Richard III

AUGUST WILHELM SCHLEGEL ON THE PLAY'S
POETICAL JUSTICE

[In this excerpt, Schlegel remarks upon Richard's lust for power
and the collusion of the audience in the making of the play's catastrophe and "the revelation of an invisible blessing or curse
which hangs over human sentiments and actions."]

The part of Richard III has become highly celebrated in England from its
having been filled by excellent performers, and this has naturally had an
influence on the admiration of the piece itself, for many readers of Shakespeare stand in want of good interpreters of the poet to understand him
properly. This admiration is certainly in every respect well founded,
though I cannot help thinking there is an injustice in considering the
three parts of *Henry the Sixth* as of little value compared with *Richard the
Third.* These four plays were undoubtedly composed in succession, as is
proved by the style and the spirit in the handling of the subject: the last is
definitely announced in the one which precedes it, and is also full of references to it: the same views run through the series; in a word, the whole
make together only one single work. Even the deep characterization of
Richard is by no means the exclusive property of the piece which bears his
name: his character is very distinctly drawn in the two last parts of *Henry
the Sixth;* nay, even his first speeches lead us already to form the most
unfavourable anticipations of his future conduct. He lowers obliquely
like a dark thundercloud on the horizon, which gradually approaches
nearer and nearer, and first pours out the devastating elements with
which it is charged when it hangs over the heads of mortals. Two of
Richard's most significant soliloquies which enable us to draw the most
important conclusions with regard to his mental temperament, are to be
found in *The Last Part of Henry the Sixth.* As to the value and the justice
of the actions to which passion impels us, we may be blind, but wickedness cannot mistake its own nature; Richard, as well as Iago, is a villain
with full consciousness. That they should say this in so many words, is
not perhaps in human nature: but the poet has the right in soliloquies to
lend a voice to the most hidden thoughts, otherwise the form of the
monologue would generally speaking, be censurable. Richard's deformity
is the expression of his internal malice, and perhaps in part the effect of it:
for where is the ugliness that would not be softened by benevolence and
openness? He, however, considers it as an iniquitous neglect of nature,
which justifies him in taking his revenge on that human society from
which it is the means of excluding him. Hence these sublime lines:

> And this word love, which graybeards call divine,
> Be resident in men like one another,
> And not in me. I am myself alone.

Wickedness is nothing but selfishness designedly unconscientious; however it can never do altogether without the form at least of morality, as this is the law of all thinking beings,—it must seek to found its depraved way of acting on something like principles. Although Richard is thoroughly acquainted with the blackness of his mind and his hellish mission, he yet endeavours to justify this to himself by a sophism: the happiness of being beloved is denied to him; what then remains to him but the happiness of ruling? All that stands in the way of this must be removed. This envy of the enjoyment of love is so much more natural in Richard, as his brother Edward, who besides preceded him in the possession of the crown, was distinguished by the nobleness and beauty of his figure, and was an almost irresistible conqueror of female hearts. Notwithstanding his pretended renunciation, Richard places his chief vanity in being able to please and win over the women, if not by his figure at least by his insinuating discourse. Shakespeare here shows us, with his accustomed acuteness of observation, that human nature, even when it is altogether decided in goodness or wickedness, is still subject to petty infirmities. Richard's favourite amusement is to ridicule others, and he possesses an eminent satirical wit. He entertains at bottom a contempt for all mankind: for he is confident of his ability to deceive them, whether as his instruments or his adversaries. In hypocrisy he is particularly fond of using religious forms, as if actuated by a desire of profaning in the service of hell the religion whose blessings he had inwardly abjured.

So much for the main features of Richard's character. The play named after him embraces also the latter part of the reign of Edward IV., in the whole a period of eight years. It exhibits all the machinations by which Richard obtained the throne, and the deeds which he perpetrated to secure himself in its possession, which lasted however but two years. Shakespeare intended that terror rather than compassion should prevail throughout this tragedy: he has rather avoided than sought the pathetic scenes which he had at command. Of all the sacrifices to Richard's lust of power, Clarence alone is put to death on the stage: his dream excites a deep horror, and proves the omnipotence of the poet's fancy: his conversation with the murderers is powerfully agitating; but the earlier crimes of Clarence merited death, although not from his brother's hand. The most innocent and unspotted sacrifices are the two princes: we see but little of them, and their murder is merely related. Anne disappears without our learning any thing farther respecting her: in marrying the murderer of her husband, she had shown a weakness almost incredible. The parts of Lord Rivers, and other friends of the queen, are of too secondary a nature to excite a powerful sympathy; Hastings, from his triumph at the fall of his friend, forfeits all title to compassion; Buckingham is the satellite of the tyrant, who is afterwards consigned by him to the axe of the executioner. In the background the widowed Queen Margaret appears as the fury of the past, who invokes a curse on the future: every calamity, which her enemies draw down on each other, is a cordial to her revengeful heart. Other female voices join, from time to time, in the lamentations and imprecations. But Richard is the soul or rather the dæmon, of the whole tragedy. He fulfils the promise which he formerly made of leading the murderous Macchiavel to school. Notwithstanding the uniform aversion with which he inspires us, he still engages us in the greatest variety of ways by his profound skill in dissimulation, his wit, his prudence, his presence of mind, his quick activity, and his valour. He fights at last against Richmond like a desperado, and dies the honourable death of a hero on the field of battle. Shakespeare could not change this historical issue, and yet it is by no means satisfactory to our moral feelings, as Lessing, when speaking of a German play on the same subject, has very judiciously remarked. How has Shakespeare solved this difficulty? By a wonderful invention he opens a prospect into the other world, and shows us Richard in his last moments already branded with the stamp of reprobation. We see Richard and Richmond in the night before the battle sleeping in their tents; the spirits of the murdered victims of the tyrant ascend in succession, and pour out their curses against him, and their blessings on his adversary. These apparitions are properly but the dreams of the two generals represented visibly. It is no doubt contrary to probability that their tents should only be separated by so small a space; but Shakespeare could reckon on poetical spectators who were ready to take the breadth of the stage for the distance between two hostile camps, if for such indulgence they were to be recompensed by beauties of so sublime a nature as this series of spectres and Richard's awakening soliloquy. The catastrophe of *Richard the Third* is, in respect to the external events, very like that of *Macbeth:* we have only to compare the thorough difference of handling them to be convinced that Shakespeare has most accurately observed poetical justice in the genuine sense of the word, that is, as signifying the revelation of an invisible blessing or curse which hangs over human sentiments and actions.

—August Wilhelm Schlegel, *Lectures on Dramatic Art and Literature,* John Black, trans., 1809.

Bruce W. Young on Parental Blessings in the Play

[Bruce W. Young is associate professor of English at Brigham Young University, where he teaches courses in Shakespeare and literary theory. Among his publications are essays on *Lear* and *The Winter's Tale* in the MLA Approaches to Teaching World Masterpieces series. In this excerpt, Young discusses the ironic effect of the blessing ritual in emphasizing "the distance between Richard and grace in any of its senses."]

The blessing ritual is mentioned three times in *Richard III* and appears mainly for ironic effect, to emphasize the distance between Richard and grace in any of its senses. The first reference, near the beginning of the play, is made by Clarence as he attempts to convince his murderers that Richard loves him:

> Tell him, when that our princely father York
> Blest his three sons with his victorious arm,
> And charg'd us from his soul to love each other,
> He little thought of this divided friendship.
> Bid Gloucester think of this, and he will weep.
>
> (I.iv.235–39)

The irony is not only that Richard has arranged for Clarence's death, but also that he would be insensible to the kind of appeal—dependent on reverence for the blessing ritual—that his brother is making.

The two remaining references to the blessing ritual are nicely balanced, one occurring about a third of the way into the play while Richard is on the rise, the other near the end of the play, just before Richard's defeat and death. In the first, Richard, already responsible for the death of his brother Clarence and soon to be responsible for the deaths of others, kneels before his mother with the pretense of seeking her grace (i.e., her favor, her beneficent influence). He says, "Humbly on my knee / I crave your blessing"; and she responds: "God bless thee, and put meekness in thy breast / Love, charity, obedience, and true duty!" Richard's reply is "Amen!" But he adds in an aside—"and make me die a good old man! / That is the butt-end of a mother's blessing. / I marvel that her Grace did leave it out" (II.ii.105–11). In the last line quoted, "Grace" is a "courtesy-title" (OED, s.v. 'grace,' II.16b). But in context, the title suggests other meanings of *grace:* "virtue," "kindness," "mercy," "beneficent influence of heaven" (Schmidt, s.v. 'grace'). The implication is that Richard's mother is a person of virtue and a source of heavenly influence. We know from his words and behavior here and elsewhere that Richard summons such images of heaven and virtue only to mock them. The thought of dying a pious death strikes him as laughable, for, as he takes pleasure in asserting, his nature is not pious—not "gracious." Such virtues as "meekness," "love, charity, obedience, and true duty," are, as he sees it, not only contrary to his nature, but contrary to his aim: namely, self-serving power, which requires an efficient ruthlessness quite opposed to the generous, merciful disposition implied by the word *grace.* Richard's appearance, too, distances him from grace. "Rudely stamp'd," "Deform'd, unfinish'd," as he himself says (I.i.16, 20), Richard lacks grace in the sense of "beauty, attraction, charm" (Schmidt, s.v. 'grace'). Indeed, the play presents his deformed body as symbolic—even as a manifestation—of his moral deformity.

Far from being merely horrifying, though, Richard's mocking of his mother's blessing allows him to forge a curiously intimate bond with his audience. It is hard to avoid laughing when he says, "I marvel that her Grace did leave it out"; it is hard to avoid admiring the wit and energy of the whole aside. And the fact that it is an aside means that we are offered the special privilege of overhearing what most on the stage do not hear. In more than one sense, we are "taken in."

But it is more than the speaker's wit and special conditions of the aside that allow Richard's seductive appeal to work its spell on us in this scene. It is easy for us, like Richard, to be put off by ceremony and by calls to "meekness" and "obedience"; it is easy, too, for us to resist expressions of love, especially when these are joined with an implied challenge to our moral standing. There is something appealing, in other words, in the very qualities that make Richard a villain, especially his resistance to pious conformity and the rational, pragmatic spirit that he has turned entirely to self-advancement. Richard is certainly no victim of what Nietzsche would later call "slave morality." He expresses no reverence for tradition or ceremony and, in fact, seems to find in these nothing more than empty forms that he can use for his own ends.

For a time, other characters share his attitude, especially Buckingham, who counters the Cardinal's objection to violating sanctuary with "You are . . . / Too ceremonious and traditional" (III.i.44–45). The play treats this antagonism toward ritual and tradition with a curious detachment. Explicit commentary and judgment are kept at a minimum (in the case I have just referred to, the Cardinal simply gives in), with the effect that we find few obstacles to fellow feeling with the villains of the play, at least on this matter of "tradition." By the end of the play we have reason enough to see Richard's attitude as deficient; in particular, his mockery of the blessing ritual—one expression of his scorn for the past and for the complex social and cosmic connections that hold the world together—helps explain his incapacity for normal or happy human relationships. But because in the course of the play we have become Richard's accomplices in some measure, the shock of understanding what his attitudes mean strikes us with even greater force.

The blessing ritual is referred to again near the end of *Richard III*; this blessing is given to Richmond "by attorney"—that is, through his stepfather—"from [his] mother" (V.iii.83). One effect of this blessing, with its prophetic wish "for Richmond's good" (line 84), is to prepare us for Richmond's victory. While the play's earlier references to the blessing ritual came when Richard was on the rise, this last one comes shortly before his fall and signals Richmond's replacing him as the play's dominant force. Because Richmond, unlike Richard, does not reject or mock his mother's blessing, the blessing serves to notify us of the normality of his relationship with his mother and to set him, as Richard's main antagonist, more sharply in contrast to the title character, whose familial relationships are anything but normal.

—Bruce W. Young, "Ritual as Grace: Parental Blessings in *Richard III, All's Well That Ends Well,* and *The Winter's Tale.*" In *True Rites and Maimed Rites: Ritual and Anti-Ritual in Shakespeare and His Age.* Linda Woodbridge and Edward Berry, eds. (Urbana, IL: Univ. of Illinois Press, 1992), pp. 174–176.

WILLIAM C. CARROLL ON RITUAL AND SUCCESSION IN THE PLAY

[William C. Carroll is professor of English at Boston University. He is the author of *The Great Feast of Language in "Love's Labour's Lost"* and *The Metamorphoses of Shakespearean Comedy.* In this excerpt, Carroll discusses the ways in which Richard seems bent on destroying all forms of law. At one point, when he has at last emptied the power and sanctity of marriage and birth rituals of all their cultural force, "he tries to crawl back inside them himself; even the empty shell of ritual is preferable to his own shape."]

Few if any forms of law in *Richard III* survive unblemished. The grisly circumstances of Richard's own birth suggest the originating transgression in natural law against "form" in general which is, contra Bacon, both "cause" and "sign" in this play. Richard himself tells us how he was

> Cheated of feature by dissembling Nature,
> Deform'd, unfinish'd, sent before my time
> Into this breathing world scarce half made up—
> And that so lamely and unfashionable
> That dogs bark at me, as I halt by them.
> (I.i.19–23)

This disruption heralds the arrival of something quite unnatural in the world, foreshadowing the "deform'd" and "unfinish'd" nature of virtually every rite of passage or social form in the play. Richard's very first victim, his brother Clarence, is done in through a hideous perversion of the sacrament of baptism: Richard tells him—as he is sent to prison—that perhaps the King "hath some intent / That you should be new christen'd in the Tower" (I.i.49–50); Clarence has already of course been "christen'd" as the fulfillment of the prophecy "which says that 'G' / Of Edward's heirs the murderer shall be" (I.i.39–40). Clarence's drowning in the malmsey-butt is not only a horrid joke on the promised christening, but perhaps also, as Anthony Hammond suggests, "a grotesque parody of the Eucharist . . . at the behest of the anti-Christ Richard . . . Clarence is 'made a sop of,' a human host soaked in wine, by murderers who call him a 'bloody minister,' debate of theology, and make comparisons of their acts with those of Pilate."

In resisting the murderers, moreover, Clarence engages them in a high-rhetorical debate about the sacred origins of authority, conducted in the theological-philosophical vocabulary of a belief system in which no one in the play actually seems to believe:

> *Cla.* I charge you, as you hope to have redemption,
> By Christ's dear blood, shed for our grievous sins,
> That you depart and lay no hands on me:
> The deed you undertake is damnable.

> *1M.*   What we will do, we do upon command.
> *2M.*   And he that hath commanded is our King.
> *Cla.*   Erroneous vassals! The great King of kings
> Hath in the table of His law commanded
> That thou shalt do no murder. Will you then
> Spurn at His edict, and fulfil a man's?
> Take heed! For He holds vengeance in His hand
> To hurl upon their heads that break His law.
>   (I.iv.178–89)

The "table of His law" has in this world already declined into the "course" and mere "form of law," where man's "edict" holds sway over God's. Redemption by Christ's blood has likewise devolved into another kind of mockery, a mechanical series of formulaic confessions by Richard's victims before their murders. In promising God's vengeance, finally, Clarence sounds eerily like Gaunt in *Richard II*, predicting divine vengeance on Richard for the murder of Woodstock. Clarence's rhetoric fails to move the murderers, in any event, who point out that he himself is "a traitor to the name of God" in his own treachery and betrayal: "How canst thou urge God's dreadful law to us, / When thou hast broke it in such dear degree?" (lines 198–99). The divinity that doth hedge a king is thus everywhere invoked but never observed.

Clarence is accused, in particular, of ripping open "the bowels of thy sovereign's son" (line 196), but in the skill of murdering children, Clarence must necessarily defer to his master in this trade, his brother. Richard's revenge for his own betrayal as a child is harsh, and in kind: his first instincts are to murder children, particularly those to whom nature has not done ill, and those for whom social relation has not been transgressed. "Tetchy and wayward" (IV.iv.169) in his own infancy, his birth "a grievous burden" to his mother, Richard quite naturally settles his hatred on those whose births were natural and noble, whose passage through this stage did not leave them deformed or unfinished. To one of Clarence's children, we learn, Richard wept (this just before they learn their father has been murdered), "And pitied me, and kindly kiss'd my cheek; / Bade me rely on him as on my father, / And he would love me dearly as a child" (II.ii.24–26). Richard follows Buckingham at the end of this scene—"I, as a child, will go by thy direction" (II.ii.53)—to take on the child of his brother Edward, now become Edward V: "So wise so young, they say, do never live long" (III.i.79). Even Richard's metaphors here suggest the "unfinish'd" curtailing of seasonal order and transition: "Short summers lightly have a forward spring" (III.i.94).

In ordering his most infamous assault against children, the Tower murders, Richard exclaims, "I wish the bastards dead" (IV.ii.18), thus justifying his order by denying the legitimacy of their succession. Tyrrel's description of the murdered princes, "this piece of ruthless butchery" (IV.iii.5), on the other hand, turns them back into "gentle babes . . . girdling one another / Within their alabaster innocent arms." They seem no less than heavenly cherubs here, as the verse waxes pastoral-poetic: "Their lips were four red roses on a stalk / And in their summer beauty kiss'd each other. / A book of prayers on their pillow lay . . . " (IV.iii.9–14). When Richard takes stock of his situation at the end of this scene, his attention focuses almost exclusively on his enemies' children, whose natural maturation and marriage he would disrupt and undermine: "The son of Clarence have I pent up close; / His daughter meanly have I match'd in marriage; / The sons of Edward sleep in Abraham's bosom" (IV.iii.36–38). Finally, when wooing Queen Elizabeth for her daughter, Richard makes an appeal now ironic and chilling, promising to begin anew the cycle of birth and maturation which he has nearly finished annihilating:

> If I have kill'd the issue of your womb,
> To quicken your increase, I will beget
> Mine issue of your blood upon your daughter.
> A grandam's name is little less in love
> Than is the doting title of a mother.

Richard then notes that grandchildren "are as children but one step below . . . of your very blood; / Of all one pain," with the single exception, he says in one of his greatest sophistries, "save for a night of groans / Endur'd of [the daughter], for whom you bid like sorrow" (IV.iv.296–304). Reducing the experience of birth to "a night of groans," Richard proleptically reveals the future pain of his own victims here. His final appeal to Elizabeth carries this nasty ambiguity to an extreme: "But in your daughter's womb I bury them [her dead children] / Where, in that nest of spicery, they will breed / Selves of themselves, to your recomforture" (IV.iv.423–25). For Richard the womb is always a tomb, the source of his birth but also the source of his imprisonment. His imagery is doubly revealing here, for Elizabeth's dead children will somehow, in her daughter's womb, reproduce incestuously and autonomously ("they will breed / Selves of themselves"). Richard's irony and bitterness run so deep that he can claim not to know "that Englishman alive / With whom my soul is any jot at odds, / More than the infant that is born tonight" (II.i.70–72). His quest to slay the first-born of the kingdom—those most likely to inherit—of course links Richard with another infamously bloody king, Herod—one also identified in tradition, as Scott Colley has demonstrated, as a "crippled, incestuous tyrant."

As with the law, the "form" of marriage is both desired and violated by Richard throughout the play. His wooing and marriage of Lady Anne, most notoriously, suggest the extent of Richard's perversions of the ritual of traditional courtship rites and the orderly process of marriage. Richard's language frequently suggests a particularly perverse transgression against marriage as well—incest:

> I'll marry Warwick's youngest daughter—
> What though I kill'd her husband and her father?
> The readiest way to make the wench amends
> Is to become her husband, and her father:
> The which will I, not all so much for love
> As for another secret close intent,
> By marrying her which I must reach unto.
>   (I.i.153–59)

In wooing Queen Elizabeth, we saw, he promised to "beget / Mine issue of your blood upon your daughter." The suggestion of incest is not only with the mother but with the daughter, for "I must be married to my brother's daughter" (IV.ii.60) in order to solidify his claim to the throne. At the same time he seeks "some mean poor gentleman, / Whom I will marry straight to Clarence' daughter" (IV.ii.53–54), who by the next scene has been "meanly . . . match'd in marriage" (IV.iii.37). In urging Queen Elizabeth to woo her daughter on his behalf, Richard urges "my mother" (IV.iv.325) to acquaint her daughter "with the sweet, silent hours of marriage joys" (IV.iv.330). The poetical alliteration here masks the most outrageous vision of marriage in the play.

Richard will even go so far in his assault on marriage as to "Infer the bastardy of Edward's children" (III.v.74) and, if necessary, allow Buckingham to tell the Mayor and citizens that Edward himself was illegitimate, and thus his own mother had violated the state and form of marriage:

> Tell them, when that my mother went with child
> Of that insatiate Edward, noble York
> My princely father then had wars in France,
> And by true computation of the time
> Found that the issue was not his-begot.
>   (III.v.85–89)

Buckingham complies by reviving the unsavory rumors of Edward's "contract with Lady Lucy, / And his contract by deputy in France" (III.vii.5–6) as well as Edward's "own bastardy" (line 9). This latter issue, Richard instructs Buckingham, is to be gingerly approached "Because, my lord, you know my mother lives" (III.v.93). This tender regard for his mother comes to an abrupt end in IV.iv, when the Duchess of York describes herself to her son as "she that might have intercepted thee—/ By strangling thee in her accursed womb" (lines 137–38).

The natural form and order of marriage and birth, then, represent for Richard what he is denied, what he desires, and what he must violate. His actions make a mockery of the power and sanctity of these rites, but no sooner has he emptied them of all cultural force, turned them inside out, than he tries to crawl back inside them himself; even the empty shell of ritual is preferable to his own shape.

—William C. Carroll, "'The Form of Law': Ritual and Succession in *Richard III.*" In *True Rites and Maimed Rites: Ritual and Anti-Ritual in Shakespeare and His Age.* Linda Woodbridge and Edward Berry, eds. (Urbana, IL: Univ. of Illinois Press, 1992), pp. 205–210.

E. Pearlman on the Invention of Richard of Gloucester

[E. (Elihu) Pearlman is author of *William Shakespeare: The History Plays.* In this excerpt, Pearlman examines how Richard's "perverse individualism" shapes a dramatic figure who can "dominate the stage with his demonism, psychological coherence, and brilliance of language."]

When Shakespeare later wrote *The Tragedy of Richard III,* he had already learned how to integrate the realistic and the symbolic. On the realistic level, throughout *Richard III* Richard's private history is a continuing concern, and the dynamics of his personal psychology and of his deeply riven family are not neglected but are set out in abundant detail. Richard is a creature of his deformity and jealousy, a character hated by his own mother and who hates all women in return. He is portrayed as having been a child whose birth was a "greeuous burthen" to his mother; who was "[t]etchy and wayward" in his infancy, "frightfull, desp'rate, wilde, and furious" as a schoolboy; and who arrived in the world (according to the outlandish canard repeated by Holinshed) "not vn-toothed." Following the precedent of the great soliloquy in *3 Henry VI,* Shakespeare supplemented so natural an account of Richard's malevolence with a second system of explanation. While *Richard III* is certainly a tragedy of unconscionable and distorted human ambition, it is also a play where the wounds of the murdered bleed again in the presence of the murderer, where the stumbling of a horse is a compelling omen, where dreams possess explanatory value, where ghosts return to influence and govern temporal events, and where prophecies are fulfilled not in a vague and general outline but in specific detail. Richard is at once the ferociously envious and warped younger brother who compensates for lost love with ambition and villainy, and also an allegorized and devilish embodiment of evil. Natural and supernatural elements come into simultaneous play at the end of the story when Richard finds himself afflicted by burgeoning guilt. When the doomed king lies in uneasy sleep on Bosworth field and is haunted by the ghosts of those he has murdered, an audience that knows Richard is a mere human mortal afflicted with naturally explicable remorse is also authorized to believe that supernatural beings have chosen a propitious moment to overthrow a satanic usurper. But at the moment of writing the hinge soliloquy in which Richard's character emerges, these innovations, though adumbrated, are still in Richard's future—just as are, in Shakespeare's future, such characters as Iago and Edmund, in which similar configurations are exploited with even greater verve and power. ⟨...⟩

The antagonism between Richard and Edward (and George) seems to have fired Shakespeare's imagination. In finding this focus, Shakespeare tapped a well of Elizabethan resentment. Except for areas in Kent which still practiced gavelkind and for sections of the Celtic marches in which tanistry had persisted, England held strictly to primogeniture. The disenfranchisement of younger brothers, and even of the "younger sons to younger brothers" whom Falstaff dimisses so glibly, was a national grievance. The sentiment that animates Thomas Wilson's cry from the heart in *The State of England, 1600* must have been shared by many a member of Shakespeare's audience: younger brothers are only allowed "that which the cat left on the malt heap, perhaps some small annuity during his life, or what please our elder brother's worship to bestow upon us if we please him and my mistress his wife." But Wilson adds that such disadvantages may provoke ambition or revenge; a younger brother might take up either letters or arms as a profession, "whereby many times we become my master elder brother's masters, or at least their betters in honour and reputation. ..." (Shakespeare himself was a first surviving child—three elder siblings had died before his birth— and nothing is known of the emotions he felt toward his younger brothers Edmund and Richard.)

None of Shakespeare's history plays stray far from the subject of antagonism between brothers. Hal's rivalry with Hotspur would be understood as a conflict between surrogate brothers even if Henry Bolingbroke had not been so tactless as to wish that the Plantagenet and Percy sons had been exchanged in cradle-clothes. Prince Hal even has a surrogate brother in the person of Poins; Poins is an underfinanced "second brother" (*2 Henry IV*, 2.2.63), Hal an older brother alienated from his natural siblings. In *2 Henry IV,* Shakespeare dwells on the contrast between the playful Prince Hal and the sober-blooded and unscrupulous John of Lancaster. Moreover, the old king's deathbed fright is the prospect of war between his sons, and the new King Henry's first concern on succeeding to the crown is to allay such apprehensions:

> Brothers, you mix your sadness with some fear.
> This is the English, not the Turkish court;
> Not Amurath an Amurath succeeds,
> But Harry Harry. ...
>
> (5.2.46–49)

The worried younger brothers must be reassured that Hal does not plan a mass murder of the sort familiar from recent Ottoman history (well known to theatrical audiences from its lurid echoes in *Selimus* and *Soliman and Perseda*).

Of all the glosses on Richard's "I haue no Brother" in the history plays, the grandest appears when Henry V inspires his troops just before the battle of Agincourt. Henry exalts the fellowship of those who will fight on St. Crispin's day and on the subject of brotherhood adopts a position that is the polar opposite of Richard's.

> We few, we happy few, we band of brothers;
> For he to-day that sheds his blood with me
> Shall be my brother; be he ne'er so vile
> This day shall gentle his condition. . . .
> *(Henry V,* 4.3.60–63)

While Richard sets himself apart even from his own brothers, King Harry proclaims a fraternity of shared pain. Harry's world is as inclusive as Richard's is exclusive, and his comprehensive vision of England is a generous alternative to the narrow and perverse individualism that makes Richard so dangerous a politician and so powerful a dramatic figure. The supersession of "I have no brother" by "we band of brothers" is a crucial marker in Shakespeare's long and epochal progress from a playwright whose initial and inherited subject was revenge to one who turned at last to reconciliation and forgiveness—to the realization that "the rarer action is / In virtue than in vengeance" (*The Tempest,* 5.1.27–28). The long journey could not begin until Shakespeare had contrived a villain who could dominate the stage with his demonism, psychological coherence, and brilliance of language.

—E. Pearlman, "The Invention of Richard of Gloucester," *Shakespeare Quarterly* 43, no. 4 (Winter 1992): pp. 424, 427–429.

Marie A. Plasse on Corporeality and the Opening of the Play

[Marie A. Plasse is associate professor of English at Merrimack College. Her work includes essays on popular culture and the study of the human body in Shakespearean drama. In this excerpt, Plasse discusses the way in which the audience's preconceptions of Richard's appearance assist Shakespeare in the presentation of the character's body as a sign of moral depravity.]

Every play necessarily depends on the corporeal medium of the actors' bodies to hold the audience's interest and to make meaning. As Michael Goldman has aptly observed, "An actor's profession and desire are to interest people with his body . . . Our response to what the actor does with his body, to the strains that are put upon it and the graces it reveals, are very strong components of our response to the play as a whole." The actor who plays Richard, however, inherits an extra charge of corporeal affect by virtue of the preconceptions his audience is likely to harbor about the body of the character. Long before Shakespeare's Richard went onstage, the image of Richard as an evil, misshapen monster was firmly established in the popular imagination. Owing chiefly to Sir Thomas More's portrait of Richard as "little of stature, ill fetured of limmes, crokebacked, his left shoulder much higher than his right, hard fauored of visage . . . malicious, wrathfull, enuious . . . a deepe dissumuler . . . not letting to kisse whom hee thought to kill," a characterization later incorporated into chronicles by Hall, Holinshed, and others, Richard's physical deformity had gained considerable notoriety by the time Shakespeare's version of him appeared. It seems likely, therefore, that many members of Shakespeare's audience would have been predisposed to pay particular attention to Richard's physical presence and to anticipate with interest the theatrical representation of his legendary deformity. What would this notorious monster look like? Sound like? What would he do?

Modern audiences, too, are likely to approach this play with preconceptions about Richard which dispose them to fix their attention on his body. The stockpile of facts, legends, and images which furnishes modern theatergoers with their vision of the character is, if anything, even larger than that from which Shakespeare's audience might have culled its notion of Richard. The ideas available for us to bring to the play include not only the legend of Richard's deformity and some knowledge of Shakespeare's sources, but also some past experience, however vague, with Shakespeare's play itself, and any number of different performances of the role, parodies, and passing references to Richard in countless other texts.

The dramaturgy of Act 1, Scene 1 of *Richard III* suggests a playwright keenly aware of and prepared to exploit his audience's preset attention to the body of the leading character by putting Richard onstage alone and giving him a forty-line speech. Simply by virtue of the amount of time required for their performance, Richard's entrance and speech virtually guarantee several moments of sustained attention from the audience, certainly enough time for Richard's physical presence to register strongly. The performance history of the play also suggests that the corporeal energies which inhere in Richard's first moments onstage are strong enough to have preoccupied actors and audiences for several centuries. In addition, the fact that Richard speaks as a prologue here, filling in past action, describing the present situation, and setting the play in motion with a frank declaration of villainous intent, would also compel the audience to be especially attentive. Richard offers information that they need as they begin to focus on the world of the play unfolding. ⟨. . .⟩

As the plot swings into action after Richard's opening monologue, incidents gradually accumulate which develop and complicate the foregrounding of the body and of corporeal signs executed in Act 1, Scene 1. Richard's clever, calculated attacks on those who block his path to the throne, for example, are repeatedly registered through an emphasis on corporeal images, both in the language and in the staging of the play. Although Richard's subtle capacity to outwit his opponents is presented as formidable and his psychological insights acute, the full measure of his power is most impressively conveyed in his relentless pursuit of and control over the bodies of his foes. Unlike Iago, another self-conscious, ambitious villain, Richard, for the most part, is not particularly interested in toying with his victims, leading them to destruction through repeated encounters, insinuations, and exhortations which occur over a long period of time. Richard's style, by and large, is much more precipitous and direct. His characteristic method of controlling and defeating his enemies is to remove them bodily from the public sphere in which he so effectively "bustles." He knocks his foes out of action by imprisoning them, one after the other, like so many forfeited chess pieces. Gradually, the body count grows.

> —Marie A. Plasse, "Corporeality and the Opening of *Richard III*." In *Entering the Maze: Shakespeare's Art of Beginning*. Robert F. Wilson Jr., ed. (New York: Peter Lang, 1995), pp. 12–15.

IAN FREDERICK MOULTON ON RICHARD'S UNRULY MASCULINITY

[In this excerpt, Moulton examines the way Richard's "deformed body figures his masculinity as both perverse and dangerous for the nation."]

The death of Richard's father at the hands of Margaret and Clifford is the occasion for a complete transformation in Shakespeare's representation of Richard. York's death comes to serve as an emblem for his son Richard's alienation from the patriarchal masculine community, and the change in Richard's social position is manifested by a precise physical change. If Warwick's army is chilled by Henry's effeminate coldness, here Richard is overcome with surfeit of masculine heat which makes it physically impossible for him to weep. This shift in Richard's humoral makeup is described in remarkable detail:

> I cannot weep, for all my body's moisture
> Scarce serves to quench my furnace-burning heart;
> Nor can my tongue unload my heart's great burden,
> For selfsame wind that I should speak withal
> Is kindling coals that fires all my breast,
> And burns me up with flames that tears would quench.
> To weep is to make less the depth of grief.
> Tears, then, for babes; blows and revenge for me!
> (3 *HVI*, 2.1.79–86)

This moment is crucial enough in Richard's development as a character for Shakespeare to recall it in detail in *Richard III*: Richard tells Anne that when his father died, though "all the standers-by had wet their cheeks / Like trees bedashed with rain—in that sad time / My manly eyes did scorn an humble tear" (*RIII*, 1.2.165–67).

In the humoral physiology of the early modern period, the human body was conceived as a "semipermeable, irrigated container" of fungible liquids—blood, sperm, bile, phlegm, tears, sweat. As John Donne asserted in a Lenten sermon of 1623, "every man is but a spunge, and but a spunge filled with teares." To be healthy, the fragile balance of liquid humors in the body had to be carefully maintained according to an economy of heat and cold which differed for men and women: men ought ideally to be relatively hot and dry, women to be moist and cold. In figuring his heart as a fiery furnace, Richard clearly describes the process by which his metabolic equilibrium is being thrown out of balance. An excess of masculine heat is parching his body: he is drying up. His inability to cry prevents his body from maintaining a healthy humoral balance.

Although throughout *Richard III* weeping is seen as characteristic of women, children, and effeminate lovers (e.g., 1.2.157–58; 2.2; 4.4.201–2), it is important to realize that weeping as such was not uniformly conceived of as unmanly in early modern culture. Just as in the patriarchal cultures of antiquity, men were traditionally permitted, even expected, to weep on just the occasion when Richard proves unable to— the death of a comrade in battle. Thus Richard's own father weeps for the death of his youngest son, crying, "These tears are my sweet Rutland's obsequies, / And every drop cries vengeance for his death" (*3 HVI*, 1.4.147–48). York's reading of his own tears as a sign of vengeance demonstrates that the dichotomy between weeping and manliness, between mourning and vengeance, is not a cultural imperative but rather a paradigm that Richard chooses to adopt.

After his father's death Richard's physical abnormality—his monstrosity—obtains inwardly as well as outwardly: his humoral imbalance, his excessive heat, is just as monstrous as his crooked back and withered arm. His physical monstrosity manifests itself as social monstrosity. While York lives, Richard's devotion to his father marks him as an orderly subject of the patriarchy; though he (and his family) are in rebellion against the monarch, Richard accepts patriarchy as such. His loyalty to the father of his family rather than to King Henry, who has failed so singularly as father of the country. But Richard's inability to mourn York's death marks a perverse turning away from patriarchal principles. Left without a father to subordinate himself to, Richard fights for himself alone. As he proudly declares after killing Henry VI,

> I have no brother, I am like no brother;
> And this word "love," which graybeards call divine,
> Be resident in men like one another
> And not in me. I am myself alone.
> (*3 HVI*, 5.6.80–83)

33

Richard believes his deformity sets him apart from others, but instead it is his aggressively masculine singularity that constitutes his monstrosity. His ambition, his prowess as a warrior, his viciousness, his cruel intelligence—the same masculine qualities that made him an asset to the Yorkists as a group—become monstrous when cut loose from the structure of bonds between male warriors which constitutes English ruling-class society. The alienation of Richard's masculinity from the patriarchal order that ought to channel its energies gives his physical deformity significance; indeed it is only after his father's death that he begins to lament his condition and to devise various explanations and genealogies for it (*3HVI*, 3.2.146–95; 5.6.68–83).

From the death of York onward, much is made in the tetralogy of Richard's deformity and his monstrous birth: he was a premature child, "an indigested and deformèd lump," born with teeth "to signify [he came] . . . to bite the world." His birth was heralded by horrid omens, and his "mother felt more than a mother's pain" (*3HVI*, 5.6.51, 54, 49). In early modern England the birth of a deformed child was inevitably seen as portentous, and in Richard's case his deformed body figures his masculinity as both perverse and dangerous for the nation. Some indication of the degree of cultural fascination with monstrous births in the late sixteenth century can be seen in such texts as Stephen Batman's lengthy tract titled *The Doome warning all men to the Iudgemente*, a compendium of "all the straunge Prodigies" and "secrete figures of Reuelations" from the time of Adam and Eve to the day the book was published. Batman casts all human history as a chronicle of reiterated warning, in which every so-called aberration of nature—from rhinoceroses to stillbirths, from floods to dreams (including Richard's dream of "deformed Images" on the evening of the battle at Bosworth)—is a divine portent filled with inescapable and terrifying significance.

—Ian Frederick Moulton, "'A Monster Great Deformed': The Unruly Masculinity of Richard III," *Shakespeare Quarterly* 47, no. 3 (Fall 1996): pp. 260–262.

Plot Summary of
Henry IV, Part 1

Act I, scene 1 opens upon Henry describing himself as weary of ruling. He intends to mount a crusade to the Holy Land as penance for his part in the murder of Richard II, but his plan is disrupted by unrest at the borders of his kingdom between the Welsh, led by Glendower, and the Scots, led by Douglas. An additional worry is his son, Prince Henry (Harry), or Hal, who seems intent on a dissipated life in the company of Sir Jack Falstaff. He wistfully compares his son to Lord Percy, called Hotspur for his impatient nature, who has been bravely engaged in the battle with the Scots. Would that Hal were so princely, he thinks. He wonders if the boys were somehow switched at birth(!) as he envies Hotspur's father, the Earl of Northumberland.

In scene 2, we learn that Hal (who will become Henry V) is not so dissolute as everyone believes. But first, he plots with Falstaff to rob travelers, a prank they have pulled before. He also plots with Poins to rob Falstaff, but with an an eye to his future position as king, when he will "imitate the sun, /. . . . And like bright metal on a sullen ground, / My reformation, glittering o'er my fault, / Shall show more goodly and attract more eyes / Than that which hath no foil to set it off. / I'll so offend, to make offense a skill; / Redeeming time when men think least I will." When he ascends the throne, his redemption from this dissipation will be all the more impressive.

Scene 3 focuses upon Hotspur, who has brought back Scottish prisoners of war and will relinquish them only on the condition that Henry agree to ransom Mortimer, Hotspur's brother-in-law. Henry refuses, calling Mortimer a traitor. The real reason for his refusal, however, is that Mortimer may have a more legitimate claim to the throne that Henry himself, a claim that Hotspur and Northumberland think valid. Hotspur refuses to relinquish his prisoners.

Hotspur, Northumberland, and Worcester (Northumberland's younger brother) discuss their problems with Henry (here called Bolingbroke, as he was known before becoming king). Hotspur criticizes his father and uncle for their subservience to Henry when it is they who helped him to achieve the throne. Hotspur is neither patient nor diplomatic, claiming that to right the wrong he feels they did by enthroning Henry would be "an easy leap, / To pluck bright honour from the pale-faced moon." With Worcester and Northumberland, Hotspur plots a rebellion that will enlist the Scottish prisoners and their leader, the archbishop of York, as well as Owen Glendower to march against Henry.

The contrast between Hotspur and Hal permeates the play. Hotspur is too impetuous ever to be a good king, as the play makes clear. Hal, on the other hand, has his father's political shrewdness and caution.

In **Act II**, scene 2 Falstaff and his band rob the travelers and, in turn, are set upon by Hal and Poins in disguise. Falstaff, as expected, runs away, leaving the spoils behind. The mood changes in scene 3 as Lady Lucy, Hotspur's wife, tries to coax from her husband the reason for his emotional distance: "What is'it," she asks, "that takes from thee / Thy stomach, pleasure, and thy golden sleep?" He tells her nothing of the rebellion plot, but the exchange is affectionate, suggesting that Hotspur is capable of love.

Meanwhile, back at the Boar's Head Tavern (scene 4), Hal and Poins tease Falstaff about the robbery. True to form, Falstaff denies his cowardice, claiming that he had been attacked by eleven men. When he learns that Hal was his attacker, Falstaff claims he had known this all along, and that he could not have defended himself: "[W]as it for me to kill the heir apparent?" he counters. When the king sends word that Hal must join him to defend against the rebels, Hal and Falstaff rehearse what Hal will tell his father about his present activities. Hal takes the role of the king, and describes Falstaff as "that father ruffian," to which Falstaff, playing the part of Hal, replies that the "king" should banish all the drinking companions save "sweet Jack Falstaff." "[B]anish plump Jack, and banish all the world," he says. Foreshadowing the future crisis between them, Hal replies, "I do, I will." Once he assumes the role expected of him and ascends the throne, he will not tolerate the likes of Falstaff.

At Glendower's castle in Wales (**Act III**, scene 1) the rebels—Hotspur, Glendower, Mortimer, and Worcester—discuss how they will divide the kingdom among themselves after they win the war. In a bitter confrontation (scene 3), Henry berates his son as a wastrel, asking him if he can be trusted to take his side against the rebels. He expresses his admiration for Hotspur, a "Mars in swathling clothes," and implies that Hal falls short by comparison. Hal pleases his father by promising to behave in a more princely manner, but we already know that he intends to fulfill his duties when he thinks it necessary.

Hal seems caught between two fathers, Henry and Falstaff, each of whom can teach him something. Falstaff's sensuality, hedonism, shrewdness, and wit are countered by Henry's sense of political responsibility and knowledge of statecraft. Although he will ultimately choose Henry's path, Hal will be a better king for his knowledge of and affection for the people.

Act IV, scene 1 opens on Hotspur's camp and the battlefield. Northumberland is ill and cannot help his son. But Hotspur means to turn this to his advantage, noting that if they can "push against a kingdom, without his help," they will prove themselves even stronger. Glendower's troops are not ready, either. Nonetheless, Hotspur is impatient for the fight and unconcerned that Hal, a "madcap," has joined Henry's forces. His attitude is that they will "die all, die merrily"—a sharp contrast to Falstaff's cowardice and Henry's caution.

In scene 2, Falstaff offers a more realistic perspective on war, telling Hal that they are just "food for powder," what we might call cannon fodder. Falstaff sees no glory in death, nor does he believe that Hotspur's increasingly anachronistic chivalric code is worth fighting for. But Falstaff is a kind of nihilist, living only for his own sensuous gratification.

Hotspur and Douglas are eager to march on the king (scene 3), although many counsel waiting until morning when their forces will be rested and more battle-ready. Sir Walter Blunt arrives with a request from Henry for a meeting. Hotspur replies that Henry has "committed wrong on wrong" by dethroning, then killing, Richard II. Hotspur and Northumberland see Mortimer, earl of March, as Richard's rightful heir. Hotspur's speech is a litany of woes, but Blunt's response is laconic: "Shall I return this answer to the king?" Hotspur checks his temper and tells Blunt that his uncle will meet with Henry in the morning. In scene 4 York confides to Sir Michael that Hotspur would be wise to accept the king's peace offer. The absence of so many of their forces seems too great a weakness to overcome.

At Henry's camp at Shrewsbury (**Act V**, scene 1), the king, Hal, his brother (Lord John of Lancaster), Blunt, and Falstaff meet Hotspur's uncle, Worcester. Henry asks his help to "unknit / This churlish knot of all-abhorred war? / And move in that obedient orb again, / where you did give a fair and natural light," implying that the rebellion has disrupted the natural order. Hal offers to fight Hotspur in single combat to settle the matter, a princely act but one the king forbids. Henry offers to pardon the rebels if they will disband.

Worcester discusses the king's offer with Vernon near the rebel camp (scene 2). Vernon wants to tell Hotspur what Henry offers, but Worcester does not believe the king will keep his word. Instead, he tells Hotspur that the king has named them all traitors and called them to battle. On the battlefield, in scene 3, many of the king's men are dressed as Henry to act as decoys during the fight. Douglas resolves simply to kill all the kings he sees. Falstaff enters alone, lamenting that almost all of his 150 men are dead. Hal enters and finds Blunt dead. Falstaff lies, telling him that he has already avenged Blunt's death. Hal pulls a bottle of sack from Falstaff's holster and, disgusted, departs. Falstaff is not ashamed, reminding us, the audience, that he would rather be alive than have such "grinning honor as Sir Walter [Blunt] hath."

Hal begins to accept his princely role as he rescues Henry from Douglas's fierce attack (Act V, scene 4), acting with honor but without Hotspur's overzealousness. "Thou hast redeemed thy lost opinion," Henry tells his son. After the king departs, the two Harrys are at last face-to-face. Hal kills Hotspur. Douglas kills Falstaff. Hal, flanked by the bodies of Hotspur and Falstaff seems poised between an outmoded chivalry and the pursuit of pleasure. He departs, having made his choice. Falstaff rises from his feigned death to remark that "the better part of valor is discretion; in which better part I have saved my life." Who would argue?

He plunges his dagger into Hotspur's thigh and lifts the dead body onto his shoulders to carry it away in triumph. Hal returns and is astonished to find his old friend alive, and more astonished to hear Falstaff's account of how he himself killed Hotspur, a lie the prince allows.

In triumph, in scene 5, Henry chastises Worcester for lying about Henry's message, and has him killed when he is unrepentant. Hal sets Douglas free as a tribute to his valor—another princely act. Henry begins laying plans for the next battle: Lord John and Westmoreland will lead half the army to meet Northumberland, while the king and Hal will march toward Wales to fight Glendower. ✤

List of Characters in
Henry IV, Part 1

Henry IV came to power in the play *Richard II* through a combination of political intrigue and rebellion; after he ascended the throne, he had Richard killed, an act that in *Henry IV, Part One,* throws into question his right to the crown. Henry is troubled by the behavior of his son Hal and by political unrest in the kingdom. He is not a particularly warm character, but his political shrewdness is a quality Hal must learn.

Henry ("Hal") is Henry IV's oldest son, the Prince of Wales. Although he will one day rule England, he spends his time with Sir John Falstaff, drinking and carousing, which causes everyone in the play to underestimate his abilities. Hal himself knows this is what people think, as demonstrated in his soliloquy in Act I, in which he says that at the right time he will change his behavior and surprise everyone. Hal must choose between the model offered by Falstaff and the model offered by his father; his choice implicitly poses the question of what makes a good ruler. Hal represents the new order; he combines political awareness with the common touch. He also must choose between the different visions of life offered by Falstaff and by Hotspur.

Sir John Falstaff is Hal's constant companion. Falstaff and his friends, all regulars at the Boar's Head Tavern in Eastcheap, are the companions that worry King Henry. Falstaff lives for pleasure, particularly food and drink. His disdain for honor and bravery put him in marked contrast to Hotspur, with whom Hal is constantly compared. Falstaff's instinct for self-preservation at all costs is demonstrated in humorous situations, as when Hal robs him, but also on the battlefield, where he plays dead to save his life. His pleasure-seeking attitude is solipsistic in the extreme: Nothing means anything to Falstaff unless it directly affects him.

Henry Percy ("Hotspur"), a member of the Percy family who helped put Henry on the throne but are now disgruntled with Henry's behavior, is Hal's counterpoint. Where Hal appears dissolute and uninterested in the condition of the state, Hotspur is vitally interested. But Hotspur is concerned only with honor and questions of chivalry; he gets what he wants by fighting rather than by thinking. The fight between Hal and Hotspur is the fight between the new order and the old; both men have princely qualities, but Hal is able to unify bravery with strategy and cunning, which Hotspur, as his name suggests, is too impatient to do. Hotspur is not an unsympathetic character; he is simply a character whose admirable qualities are outdated.

Henry Percy, earl of Northumberland, is Hotspur's father and one of the rebellion leaders. Henry IV admits to being jealous of Northumberland because Hotspur is, at least in the first three acts of the play, a more princely character than Hal.

Archibald, earl of Douglas, another rebel leader, is as impatient for battle as Hotspur. Douglas fights so valiantly during the battle that although he is captured, Hal has him set free in tribute to his valor.

Edmund Mortimer, earl of March, is fighting the Welsh when he is captured by Glendower. He marries Glendower's daughter and joins the rebel forces; it is Henry's refusal to ransom Mortimer that initially triggers Hotspur's anger.

Owen Glendower is the leader of the Welsh tribes and a coconspirator; he and Northumberland work together to try to curb Hotspur's impatience.

Poins, Gadshill, Peto, Bardolph are all friends of Hal's who frequent the Boar's Head Tavern with Falstaff. ❀

Critical Views on
Henry IV, Part 1

ROBERT N. WATSON ON KING HENRY'S GUILT AND HAL'S INCORRIGIBILITY

[Robert N. Watson, a professor of English at Harvard University, is the author of *Shakespeare and the Hazards of Ambition* (1984), from which the following extract is taken. Here, Watson asserts that King Henry sees a divine justice in Hal's misbehavior—a punishment for his own usurpation of the throne.]

Act three, scene two, of *1 Henry IV* begins with Henry's interpreting Hal's misbehavior as a divine punishment for his own misdeeds. Though Henry, as usual, pretends to be slightly uncertain what his own crime might have been, a son's rebellious refusal to rise to the level of his royal blood would be an entirely appropriate rebuke to his father's insistence on rising to claim that royal heritage. The psychoanalytic maxim that the bad son has bad sons, and the physical maxim that what goes up must come down, both work to subvert Henry's hopes for a royal heir:

> I know not whether God will have it so
> For some displeasing service I have done,
> That in his secret doom, out of my blood,
> He'll breed revengement and a scourge for me;
> But thou dost in thy passages of life
> Make me believe that thou art only mark'd
> For the hot vengeance, and the rod of heaven,
> To punish my mistreadings. Tell me else,
> Could such inordinate and low desires,
> Such poor, such bare, such lewd, such mean attempts,
> Such barren pleasures, rude society,
> As thou art match'd withal and grafted to,
> Accompany the greatness of thy blood,
> And hold their level with thy princely heart?
> (3.2.4–17)

This insistence on blood finding its own level may be Henry's effort to bluster away the fact that "his blood was poor" until he stepped "a little higher than his vow" and usurped Richard's throne (4.3.75–76). Hal's "affections" may indeed "hold a wing / Quite from the flight of all thy ancestors," making him "almost an alien to the hearts / Of all the court and princes of my blood" (3.2.29–35), but Henry is also on an errant flight from his hereditary place. The system rights itself from within: in the very act of being a punitively bad son to Henry, Hal is said to resemble Richard, to stand "in that very line" of the man whose right it was to place his likeness on the throne (3.2.85–94).

As Henry becomes caught up in the excitement of scolding his son, his language reveals a recognition that this throne is actually founded on such externalities as costume rather than such internalities as blood. He boasts of clothing himself in the simulation of an inward virtue, and of maintaining his person as if it were a borrowed garment: he won the people's affection when he "dress'd myself in such humility / That I did pluck allegiance from men's hearts," yet retained their respect by keeping "my person fresh and new, / My presence like a robe pontifical . . ." (3.2.51–56). Marvell's warning to Cromwell in the "Horation Ode" that "The same arts that did gain / A power must it maintain" seems applicable to Henry here: he discovers that the kingship gained by replacing a natural identity with an artificial one, replacing a person with a garment, can only be maintained by his remaining a polished costume rather than an authentic human being.

The redefinition of kingship implicit in Henry's usurpation is inextricably linked to a redefinition of identity, and one result is that not only Hal, but Sir Walter Blunt, and even Jack Falstaff, can play the role of King Henry IV with some success (2.4, 5.3). If Hal is what his father here calls him abusively, "the shadow of succession," there is good reason for it (3.2.99). Even Hal's promise that he "shall hereafter . . . / Be more myself" (3.2.93) has ironic overtones as a response to his father's criticisms, since Henry has just finished arguing that he won the throne by retaining an artificial self, or at least an artificial distance from himself. Whether it is Hal's or Shakespeare's, Henry's effort to define a true heir is trapped in a contradiction of his own making.

> —Robert N. Watson, *Shakespeare and the Hazards of Ambition*
> (Cambridge, MA: Harvard Univ. Press, 1984), pp. 55–56.

GRAHAM HOLDERNESS ON FALSTAFF AS A POLITICAL AND MORAL FOIL TO THE KING

> [Graham Holderness, dean of cultural and historical studies at the University of Hertfordshire, England, has written *Shakespeare's Myth* (1988), *Shakespeare Out of Court: Drama-tizations of Court Society* (1990), and *The Politics of Theatre and Drama* (1992). In this extract from *Shakespeare's History* (1985), Holderness sees Falstaff as a foil to the conventions of the English sovereign.]

It is commonplace that the figure of Falstaff, or the 'world' that figure inhabits or creates, constitutes some kind of internal *opposition* to the ethical conventions, political priorities and structures of authority and power embodied in the sovereign hegemony of king, prince and court: the state. Falstaff is at the centre of a popular comic history, located within the deterministic framework of the chronicle-history play, which challenges and subverts the imperatives of necessitarian historiography; and it is important to stress that the chronicle-history frame is qualified and criticised, not simply by the free play of Shakespeare's 'wonderful' intelligence on the underlying issues, but by a confrontation of different dramatic discourses within the drama, a confrontation which brings into play genuinely historical tensions and contradictions, drawn both from Shakespeare's own time and from the reconstructed time of the historical past.

The kind of 'opposition' represented by Falstaff is often compared with other oppositional tendencies which challenge the state in these plays: Falstaff's moral rebelliousness and illegality are seen as analogous to those forces of political subversion—the rebellion of the Percies and the Archbishop of York's conspiracy—which shake the stability of the Lancastrian dynasty. But though moral riotousness and political opposition are often arbitrarily connected by hostile propaganda, a state which ruthlessly suppresses the latter often finds space for the former—regarded perhaps as the legitimate exercise of freedom guaranteed to a despotic ruling class by the 'stability' of its government (e.g. the court of the Stuarts). It has been recognised that the revelry and satire of Falstaff constitute kinds of social practice which were afforded a legitimate space in medieval culture. Medieval European hierarchies, secular and ecclesiastical, sought to preserve the rigidity of their social relations, to control and incorporate internal tensions and oppositions, by allowing, at fixed times, temporary suspensions of rule, order and precedence: festive holidays in which moral freedom and opposition to political authority, the flouting of moral conventions and the inversion of ordinary social structures, were allowed to flourish. These periods of temporary suspension were closely analogous to, possibly related back to, religious practices of antiquity:

> Many peoples have been used to observe an annual period of license, when the customary restraints of law and morality are thrown aside, when the whole population give themselves up to extravagant mirth and jollity, and when the darker passions find a vent which would never be allowed them in the more staid and sober course of ordinary life. Such outbursts of the pent-up forces of human nature, too often degenerating into wild orgies of lust and crime, occur most commonly at the end of the year, are frequently associated . . . with one or other of the agricultural seasons, especially with the time of sowing or of harvests. (Sir James George Frazer, *The Golden Bough*)

Dance, song, feasting, moral freedom, were a natural element of most pre-Christian European religions, and were sternly condemned as unchristian, immoral licence by zealous and reforming Christian clerics, from the early Church fathers (who attacked the Roman Saturnalia) to the sixteenth-century Puritans. More generally they were modified, and incorporated into Christian observance (in the same way as the more prudent and discerning Christian missionaries tried to *adapt* rather than supplant the beliefs of those they wished to convert), so that the pagan fertility myths of the Mummers' Play became a Christmas or Springtime celebration. Such social practices were far from being simply a period of release, with bouts of drinking and lust and frenzied dancing: they were often characterised by a specific ritual shape, involving the suspension of ordinary structures of authority. The Roman Saturnalia reveals a clear ritual structure within the general surrender to appetite and passion: within it social relationships were not merely suspended but *inverted:*

> Now of all these periods of licence the one which is best known and which in modern languages has given its name to the rest, is the Saturnalia ... no feature of the festival is more remarkable, nothing in it seems to have struck the ancients themselves more than the licence granted to slaves at this time. The distinction between the free and servile classes was temporarily abolished. The slave might rail at his master, intoxicate himself like his betters, sit down at table with them, and not even a word of reproof would be administered to him for conduct which at any other season might have been punished with stripes, imprisonment, or death. Nay, more, masters actually changed places with their slaves and waited on them at table; and not till the serf had done eating and drinking was the board cleared and dinner set for his master. (Frazer)

The custom was called the saturnalian because it purported to be a temporary imitation of the 'Golden Age' society of peace, fertility, freedom and common wealth, without private property or slavery presided over by the God Saturn: 'The Saturnalia passed for nothing more or less than a temporary revival of restoration of the reign of that merry monarch'. The nostalgic sentimentalism of Roman patricians and the utopian longings of their slaves met on the common ground of saturnalian revelry and ritual: a clear acknowledgment that such a society must have been preferable to the present order, co-existed with a more pragmatic sense of the essentially limited nature of human ideals and aspirations, a sad recognition that 'order' (i.e. the contemporary state) can be suspended, but never, in practice, abolished or transformed. So the Saturnalia, and the associated rituals of medieval Europe, were

> ... an interregnum during which the customary restraints of law and morality are suspended and the ordinary rulers abdicate their authority in favour of a temporary regent, a sort of puppet king, who bears a more or less indefinite, capricious and precarious sway over a community given up for a time to riot, turbulence and disorder. (Frazer)

Similar customs are visible in later English folk-ceremonies by which the rural people celebrated spring or summer: Festivities in praise of fertility would involve the election of a mock ruler—a 'May King', a 'Summer Lord', a 'Mock Mayor'—or a King and Queen whose mock marriage would seem to symbolise some ancient myth of fertility. Such festivities, it is suspected, would probably include the exercise of practical fertility among the celebrants: 'It may be taken for granted that the summer festivals knew from the beginning that element of sexual licence which fourteen centuries of Christianity have not wholly been able to banish.' (E. K. Chambers, *The Medieval Stage*)

—Graham Holderness, *Shakespeare's History* (New York: St. Martin's Press, 1985), pp. 79–82.

Paul N. Siegel on Class Distinctions in *Part 1*

[Paul N. Siegel is a former professor of English at Long Island University in Brooklyn, New York. He has written voluminously on Shakespeare, including such books as *Shakespearean Tragedy and the Elizabethan Compromise* (1957) and *Shakespeare in His Time and Ours* (1968). In this extract from his Marxist interpretation of Shakespeare, Siegel examines the social and economic differences between Hotspur and Hal.]

The contrast in Tudor times between the old feudalistic aristocracy and the new aristocracy is best exemplified by the opposition between Hotspur and Hal. To repeat partially what I have said elsewhere,

> "Hotspur is a figure representative of the Elizabethan period as well as of the feudal past. . . . Hotspur's concept of honor (the most dedicated of whom were members of the old aristocracy in Elizabeth's court) who argued, according to Bryskett, that ' . . . a man for cause of honour may arm himself against his country.' Full of the sense of his family's 'nobility and power,' he feels that Henry has disgraced it and seeks to avenge the family honor, urging his father and uncle to 'redeem / your banished honors' and 'revenge the jeering and disdained contempt / Of this proud king' (I,iii,170–82). . . . Hotspur has the old feudal contempt of the humanistic virtues of the gentleman . . . [He] is not the man for what he calls 'mincing poetry' (III,i,34). Hunting and war are his pursuits. . . . In killing Hotspur, Hal, who has 'a truant been to chivalry,' (V,i,94) takes over Hotspur's chivalric virtues, but he purges them of their accompanying faults. He is not concerned, as is Hotspur, who could brook no 'corrival,' (I,iii,205) with a reputation of preeminent valor, but rather concerned with the honor that comes from

doing public service, an honor that in his speech before Agincourt he calls upon the commonest soldier to share with him."

The bourgeoisie, whom Hotspur regards with contempt (3.1.251–54), is an intermittently perceived force throughout the plays. The significance of its support of Bolingbroke has already been examined. To Green's statement that the king's favorites are hated by those who "love not the King," Bagot replies (2.2.128–130), "And that is the wavering commons, for their love / Lies in their purses, and whoso empties them / By so much fills their hearts with deadly hate." The "wavering commons" often is decisive, at least for the moment, in the struggle of the rival houses. "Trust me, my lord," says Warwick, the "kingmaker" (*3 Henry VI*, 4.2.1–2), after having switched from Edward IV to Henry VI, "all hitherto goes well; / The common people by numbers swarm to us."

The bourgeoisie is primarily concerned with two things: the relief from taxes of which Bagot speaks and the maintenance of a strong central government that would put down disorders and protect the flow of trade. The Bishop of Winchester, the great uncle of the king, vying with Humphrey of Gloucester, uncle of the King and Protector of the realm, seeks to incite the Lord Mayor of London against him by saying (*1 Henry VI*, 1.3.62–64), "Here's Gloucester, a foe to citizens, / One that still motions war and never peace, / O'ercharging your free purses with large fines." The Lord Mayor's attitude toward these mighty ones, whose retainers have engaged in an altercation that has raised an uproar, is one of a "plague on both your houses": "Fie, lords! that you, being supreme magistrates, / Thus contumeliously should break the peace! (57–58). He proclaims that all those who have engaged in this disturbance "against God's peace and the king's" (75) must disperse immediately and henceforth not wear weapons, threatening to call out the apprentices from their shops to assist the city officers if the combatants do not leave the scene. The strength of the bourgeoisie here apparent is even more clearly seen in the fact that Richard III feels that he needs the support of the Lord Mayor and the leading citizens, the commercial oligarchy of London, before he can be crowned king.

Shakespeare, then does more than show the changing relationship between monarchy, aristocracy, and bourgeoisie and the evolution of each in the historical period he is depicting. He shows the changes in his own time and even foreshadows the time when the bourgeoisie and its allies will overthrow a Stuart king.

—Paul N. Siegel, *Shakespeare's English and Roman History Plays: A Marxist Approach* (Rutherford, NJ: Fairleigh Dickinson Univ. Press, 1986), pp. 76–77.

PAUL M. CUBETA ON FALSTAFF'S CONVENIENT DEATHS

[Paul M. Cubeta is college professor of humanities and director of the Bread Loaf School of English at Middlebury College. He has edited *Twentieth Century Interpretations of Richard II* (1971). In this extract, Cubeta explores the many deaths and resurrections of Falstaff throughout the Henriad.]

Once the historical myths and dramatic concerns of *The Henriad* served by Falstaff's comic vision have been resolved by his legendary repudiation, Falstaff the character can no longer exist: "Reply not to me with a foolborn jest" (Shakespeare, *2H4* V.v.55). On that command to silence, the newly crowned king has destroyed his fool and jester. Falstaff could undergo a mock-magical death and resurrection at the end of *1 Henry IV,* and he essentially "dies of a sweat" at the end of *2 Henry IV* when he races recklessly to Westminster Abbey "to stand stain'd with travel, and sweating with desire to see" Hal newly crowned (V.v.24–25). But Falstaff the man cannot be dismissed or lie forgotten in Fleet Prison, abandoned by king and playwright. The Shakespearean investment in the saving grace of that comic spirit in his Lancastrian world has been too great. And so in *Henry V* he redeems Epilogue's promise in *2 Henry IV* to continue the story "with Sir John in it" (Epi., 28) with a vividly realized, yet non-existent death scene, both comic and pathetic, private and demonstrated, dedicated to the spirit of Falstaff the man.

Never allowed securely to grasp this protean giant even when his comic imagination and ironic vision die, the audience participated in the immediacy and intensity of the deathbed scene but not by observing those who stand at Falstaff's bedside. Simultaneously the audience is kept at double distance from the mystery of Falstaff's dying thoughts. Instead of sentimental farewell in the cold, pragmatic Lancastrian world, Shakespeare seeks instead a resolution in which tragedy and comedy, doubt and belief, clarity and confusion are bound in a manner historically appropriate, morally satisfying, and psychologically dazzling. The theatrical gamble of creating a character by not creating him, of giving him life by destroying him yields the most memorable scene of the play.

To achieve the dense texture of this recollected deathbed scene, Shakespeare does not turn to his usual source for things even vaguely Falstaffian in *The Henriad—The Famous Victories of Henry V* (1598). In the life of Falstaff, Shakespeare has embodied rituals, folktales, conventions, festivals as familiar to an Elizabethan audience as those he may now be suggestively recalling in the medieval and Renaissance tradition of *ars moriendi,* or the art of dying. To design a coherent structure and meaning to Falstaff's dying moments of introspection and memory, which appear as merely broken, delirious fragments, Shakespeare may also give Falstaff the occasion to attempt a private meditation on his life in the manner of a Renaissance meditation for Wednesday night.

Reported in an intensely moving yet uncertain retelling, Falstaff's mode of dying is as mysterious and as hauntingly perplexing as any circumstance in his life. The only words directly attributed to him, the great inventor of language, are "God, God, God!" (*H5* II.iii.19). But what this punster, this parodist and unparalleled player with the rhythms of spoken language, means or what tone the repetitions are spoken in is not ours to hear. The challenger of the moral, social, political, and religious values on which civilization rests dies with a word, the Word, on which pun cannot prevail. Like his heart, which Pistol avers, was "fracted and corroborate" (II.i.124), the scene recollecting Falstaff's death is a kind of transitory memorial moment, broken, unfocused, contradictory, unchronological and impossible to recreate for even their listeners by his bedside mourners, who are then about to be swept up into events in France and propelled to their own deaths.

—Paul M. Cubeta, "Falstaff and the Art of Dying," *Studies in English Literature 1500–1900* 27, no. 2 (Spring 1987): pp. 197–198.

ALEXANDER LEGGATT ON DECEPTION IN *HENRY IV, PART 1*

[Alexander Leggatt, a professor of English at the University of Toronto, is the author of *Shakespeare's Political Drama: The History Plays and the Roman Plays* (1988), from which the following extract is taken. Here, Leggatt comments on Shakespeare's use of deception in *Henry IV, Part One*, with the result that nothing in the play is as it seems.]

The rebels are concerned with appearances, no less than the King and his son, and this concern replaces the simpler aggressiveness that drove the rebels of *Henry VI*. When Hotspur promises his colleagues,

> yet time serves wherein you may redeem
> Your banish'd honours, and restore yourselves
> Into the good thoughts of the world again.
> (Pt 1, I.iii.178–80)

we catch echoes from the end of the previous scene, Hal's soliloquy announcing his strategy. Hotspur even uses two of Hal's key words 'redeem' and 'time' (cf. I.ii.212). The rebels' calculations before Shrewsbury include considerations of reputation: Worcester thinks Northumberland's absence will make the rebellion look bad; Hotspur argues it will make it look better, showing they can carry on without his help. The anxiety behind these calculations shows that the world of appearances demands tricky manoeuvring; Hotspur says he would praise Douglas properly 'If speaking truth / In this fine age were not thought flattery' (IV.i.1–2). Besides kingship, there are other kinds of coinage that can be debased. Moreover, the characters' attempts to master appearances are complicated by the fact that they are not in a single world where everyone speaks the same language, but in a fragmented one. This is no longer the tight stage community of *Richard II,* in which all eyes could be fixed on one figure; there, no one, down to the meanest gardener or groom, was excluded from the circle of attention centred on Richard. The world of *Henry IV,* on the other hand, is widely dispersed and richly varied. When Sir Walter Blunt appears in the first scene 'Stain'd with the variation of each soil / Betwixt the Holmedon and this seat of ours' (I.i.64–5), the lines evoke the physical variety of the land, and anticipate the play's treatment of other kinds of variety. No single image can stand, as did the sea-walled garden of the earlier play, for the entire nation. Similarly, when Mortimer complains, 'My wife can speak no English, I no Welsh' (III.i.187), this is a simple reflection of a general problem; in other ways, as we shall see, characters in *Henry IV* do not speak each other's languages. (Shakespeare is not just making a cheap joke about political marriages here; through the barrier imposed by language we see the affection of a couple who really wish they *could* speak to each other.)

Misinformation is a recurring motif. Part 2 opens under the aegis of the presenter Rumour with a totally garbled version of the ending of the previous play. Characters are always complaining of being misunderstood or misquoted. In the controversy over whatever Hotspur denied the King his prisoners, Northumberland claims they 'Were . . . not with such strength deny'd / As is deliver'd to your Majesty' (Pt 1, I.iii.24–5), while Hotspur flatly declares, 'My liege, I did deny no prisoners' (I.iii.28), only to admit later that he cannot remember what he said (I.iii.51–2). Hal blames his troubles with his father on 'many tales devis'd . . . By smiling pickthanks, and base newsmongers' (III.ii.23–5), and having rescued him at Shrewsbury declares, 'O God, they did me too much injury / That ever said I hearken'd for your death' (V.iv.50–1). Worcester is wary of any accommodation with the King, because 'Look how we can, or sad or merrily, / Interpretation will misquote our looks' (V.ii.12–13). By the time John of Lancaster assures the rebels at Gaultree, 'My father's purposes have been mistook' (Pt 2, IV.ii.56), the complaint has become a regular part of political discourse, and they believe it.

This is a world, then, in which appearances matter, and are not to be trusted. At its centre is the counterfeit king who is the only king England has. He is no longer the quietly expert politician of *Richard II.* At the opening of Part 1 he appears surrounded with his nobles, a familiar image of power and authority, but his first words are 'So shaken as we are, so wan with care' (Pt 1, I.i.1). He goes on to promise domestic peace and harmony:

> No more the thirsty entrance of this soil
> Shall daub her lips with her own children's blood,
> No more shall trenching war channel her fields,

> Nor bruise her flow'rets with the armed hoofs
> Or hostile paces.
>
> (Pt 1, I.i.5–9)

He sounds like Richmond at the end of *Richard III;* but the promises are all negative, and the placing of the speech at the beginning of the play makes it vulnerable. Plays do not *begin* with reconciliation and harmony; the expectations built into the dramatic form itself sabotage Henry's vision. Richard of Gloucester also began his play announcing peace, but his announcement was frankly ironic, and he was in control of the irony as Henry is not. Elsewhere Henry shows executive firmness and strength of will. But the tact he demonstrated in dealing with the York family in *Richard II* has deserted him, or he no longer bothers to exercise it, in dealing with the Percies. He loses his temper with Worcester and orders him out, cutting off Northumberland in midsentence as he does so (I.iii.10–21). When Blunt proposes a reconciliation, Henry will have none of it; he wants, and gets, a confrontation (I.iii.69–91). This may be sound strategy in the long run, but the initial impression is of a man whose nerves are on edge. He has also a curious capacity for seeing the bad side even of good news. Told that Hotspur has won a victory on his behalf, he reflects gloomily on the contrast between Hotspur and his son (I.i.77–85). This deepens in Part 2 into a terrible pessimism, a belief that it is better not to be born at all. If one could 'read the book of fate, / And see the revolution of the times' (Pt 2, III.i.45–6), then

> The happiest youth, viewing his progress through,
> What perils past, what crosses to ensure,
> Would shut the book and sit him down and die.
>
> (Pt 2, III.i.54–6)

Yet his torments are different from those of Richard III on the eve of Bosworth. Richard suffered a sharp and specific guilt; Henry, a deep but curiously unfocused *malaise.* Richard is haunted by his victims and tormented by his deeds; Henry is denied, or denies himself, such moral clarity. If he feels guilty he does not at this point say so.

For one thing—and this reflects the more realistic idiom of this play—Henry does not sense around him the supernatural framework that Richard sees so clearly. He recalls Richard II's prophecy that Northumberland would betray him, but seems to accept Warwick's analysis of it. Richard, like Henry VI, has turned out to be a true prophet. But, while Henry's accuracy can be attributed only to supernatural inspiration, Richard's (Warwick argues) was simply an intelligent observation of the principles of political behaviour; anyone who studies the past carefully can make a fair stab at predicting the future (Pt 2, III.i.80–92). In place of Richard III's flamboyant defiance of his conscience, we hear Henry's quiet 'Are these things then necessities? / Then let us meet them like necessities' (Pt 2, III.i.92–3). As we would expect, there is nothing supernatural in his view of kingship. It is, for him, an office to be earned; his persistent habit of comparing Hal with Hotspur leads to one of his most characteristic utterances:

> Now by my sceptre, and my soul to boot,
> He hath more worthy interest to the state
> Than thou the shadow of succession.
> For of no right, nor colour like to right,
> He doth fill fields with harness in the realm.
>
> (Pt 1, III.ii.97–101)

To reinforce this pragmatic view by swearing on his sceptre and his soul is another of Henry's unconscious ironies. In Part 2 we see what the crown means to him: a possession to be laid on his pillow, like a child's favourite toy. As York in *2 Henry VI* described himself as 'the silly owner of the goods' (I.i.226) and thus destroyed the dignity of his claim, the language of Henry's rebuke to Hal for stealing the crown is that of a middle-class father whose son has broken into the cashbox: 'How quickly nature falls into revolt / When gold becomes her object!' (Pt 2, IV.v.65–6). Though he predicts that the orderly succession from father to son will settle the dynastic problem, he also warns Hal that he will have to work to keep his position: 'all my friends, which thou must make thy friends, / Have but their stings and teeth newly ta'en out' (Pt 2, IV.v.204–5). (This is a sad revelation of what the word 'friend' means in politics.)

—Alexander Leggatt, *Shakespeare's Political Drama: The History Plays and the Roman Plays* (London: Routledge, 1988), pp. 78–81.

◈

RALPH BERRY ON SOCIAL LIFE IN *PART 1*

[Ralph Berry, a professor of English at Florida State University, has written *The Art of John Webster* (1972) and *Shakespearean Structures* (1981). In this extract from *Shakespeare and Social Class* (1988), Berry contrasts the portrayal of social class in *Henry IV, Part 1,* with that of *Richard II.*]

The land is no longer defined in terms of its (ailing) ruler. Instead, the sprawling, autonomous vitality of the people is everywhere. This is epic drama, and one can do worse than touch it first at the small scene with the Carriers in the Rochester inn-yard. Here are the realities of work, early starts, the insanitary habits of the English, things going wrong, fleas, damp provender, livestock to be cared for, the absence of the people who used to see that things worked, the bustle and exhilaration of the early morning. The passing of Robin Ostler is lamented, no doubt as a Homeric formula: "Poor fellow never joyed since the price of oats rose, it was the death of him" (2.1.11–12). The extraordinary sense of life as it is lived, outside the subjectivities of the main personages, is everywhere. We even know the breakfast order of the travelers who "call for eggs and butter." Can reality be more pointed than that?

The play cannot be seen simply as The Education of a Prince, or The Adventures of Jack Falstaff. The major characters grow out of the teeming life all around, who all sense this outside world of classes, types, and humanity at large. Simply to list occupations and functionaries takes a little space: burgomaster, underskinker, vintner, grandjuror, franklin, clerk, sheriff, chamberlain, hangman, drawer, weaver, factor, inn-keeper, auditor. Of this world of beings and types, Falstaff knows a great deal, and Hal picks up a great deal. The play traces Hal's learning curve.

Something of this comes out in the prologue to the tavern scene. Hal becomes a field worker specializing in language, a cultural anthropologist among a tribe virtually unknown to him. His visit to the cellar, at the invitation of the drawers, has impressed him. People are usually impressed by a tour of the cellar. Hal has encountered the drinking habits of the drawers—"when you breathe in your watering they cry 'Hem!' and bid you play it off" and concludes that "I am so good a proficient in one quarter of an hour that I can drink with any tinker in his own language during my life" (2.4.16–19). This might be an overestimate. Hal has fallen into the classic trap of the anthropologist, who contaminates the data by being there to record it. The Carriers, in the presence of nobody but each other, speak a far more vivid and resourceful language than the drawers in the presence of the prince.

Still, they add to the Prince's experience. The prime virtue of Hal is that he is prepared to experiment with roles, while retaining his identity. This is superbly symbolized in the play scene with Falstaff, when Hal first takes on the role of the Prince, then of the King himself. That, of course, is the role that most expresses him: "*I'll play my father*" (2.4.419). But just as Hal has seemed an undergraduate learning drinking practices, he puts on years in the encounter with the Sheriff who interrupts the play world. It is a neat cameo of a police inquiry, in which the detective must enter a house of multiple repute and discreetly interrogate a highly placed individual. The dangerous tensions of the matter are scrupulously depicted: the Prince may not deal with the situation via a simple discharge of vehemence; the official does his duty, but may not press it too hard. Both men tread a fine line, as the Prince finds a formula that the Sheriff can accept:

> The man I do assure you is not here,
> For I myself at this time have employed him
> [a pause, surely, for the following "And" is suggestive]
> And Sheriff, I will engage my word to thee,
> That I will by tomorrow dinnertime
> Send him to answer thee, or any man.
>
> (2.4.494–98)

It is an astonishingly mature performance. The ambivalent position of the Prince of Wales is turned to dramatic advantage: Shakespeare shows a young man not yet invested in the authority that will be his, having to deal with all social classes from tinkers to the Lord Chief Justice. Con men, friends, offers, criticism, traps, he has to surmount them all. It is an education, and Hal devours it.

Hotspur, evidently, is a different story. The point about Hotspur is not that he is stupid, but that he might just as well be. There's an archaism, a resistance to learning in his mentality that makes him functionally obsolete—not to mention, dead. Dramatically, Shakespeare has solved the problem of *Henry VI:* how does one make attractive and interesting a representative of the quarrelsome nobility that swamps the dramatis personae? He creates an enormously vital, likeable young man, hotheaded to a fault, who considers his resistance to all forms of challenge as the absolute imperative of identity. The class governs the individual. There is nothing in Hotspur of the wary adaptability of Hal, evidence of a species headed for survival and progress.

—Ralph Berry, *Shakespeare and Social Class* (Atlantic Highlands, NJ: Humanities Press, 1988), pp. 77–79.

BARBARA HODGDON ON FALSTAFF'S FEMININE CHARACTERISTICS

[Barbara Hodgdon is a professor of English at Drake University and the author of a study of *Henry IV, Part Two* (1993). In this extract from *The End Crowns All* (1991), a book on Shakespeare's history plays, Hodgdon discusses the exclusion of women in *Henry IV, Part One*, with the results that Falstaff gains some feminine characteristics.]

Unlike Shakespeare's earlier histories, where conflict centers on genealogical descent in a struggle for the crown's rightful ownership, *1 Henry IV* positions the Percy-Northumberland rebellion against the state so that it serves Hal's mimetic rivalry with Hotspur as well as that between his authentic and counterfeit fathers, Henry IV and Falstaff. In this extremely limited gender economy, structured by a desire for the male other that takes the form of aggression, women are positioned at history's margins: unnecessary to prove or deny Hal's or Hotspur's legitimacy (as, for instance, in *King John*), they simply delay historical time. Only the rebel leaders—Hotspur and Lord Mortimer—have wives, whose presence functions primarily to separate public from private domains and, by proving their husbands' heterosexuality, deflects the homoerotic into the homosocial; says Hotspur, "This is no world / To play with mammets or to tilt with lips" (2.3.87–88), nor has he time to listen to the Welsh lady sing (3.1.234).

In their resistance to the male chivalric project, Kate Percy and Glendower's daughter are kin to Falstaff, a more substantial image of feminine "misrule," who lies within the tavern space, together with thieves, swaggerers, a Hostess-landlady, and "gentlewomen" who, it is said, "live honestly by the prick of their needles" (*Henry V,* 2.1.31–32). Although within the Oedipal narrative, Falstaff figures as Hal's surrogate father, he is coded in feminine, maternal terms: his fat belly is the masculine counterpart of the pregnant woman; his Rabelaisian excesses of food and drink make him the Carnival antithesis to Henry IV's ascetic Lenten identity and his world of religious penance, bent as Henry IV is on expiating personal as well as national guilt with a crusade. It is Falstaff who accuses Hal of being the king's bastard son, and Hal, too, imagines him as female when, just before baiting Falstaff about his Gadshill cowardice and with Hotspur circulating in his mind and in his talk, he thinks himself into playing Percy and "that damned brawn" into "Dame Mortimer his wife" (2.4.104–5). That "play extempore" is then transformed into one where the roles of king and son become interchangeable, shared between Falstaff and Hal, and where women have no place: Falstaff's first "command" as "father-king" is "convey my tristful queen" (2.4.375).

But perhaps the most telling of Falstaff's multiform female guises of misrule is his association with Queen Elizabeth's virgin identity: "Let us be Diana's foresters, gentlemen of the shade, minions of the moon; and let men say we be men of good government, being governed as the sea is, by our noble and chaste mistress the moon" (1.2.23–27). Desiring to undertake something like Essex's role in the annual Accession Day Tourneys that celebrated Elizabeth's powerfully mythic, theatricalized presence, his fantasy of social order would steal and invert Essex's chivalric image—echoed in Hotspur's "easy leap / To pluck bright honor from the pale-faced moon" (1.3.201–2)—in order to recode his own body. Chivalry's daytime, however, cannot admit an aging, corpulent "squire of the night's body," whose *2 Henry IV* counterpart, mentioned in passing, is Shallow's "bona roba," Jane Nightwork (3.2.188). Even Hal, "a truant to chivalry" and the "shadow" of his father's succession (5.1.94), must transform himself to look the part of a May lord, "Ris[ing] from the ground like feathered Mercury . . . / As if an angel dropped down from the clouds," in order to confront Hotspur, a "Mars in swaddling clothes," the "king of honor" (4.1.106–8; 3.2.112; 4.1.10). And although Sir John's body is also capable of metamorphosis, his transformations, and the codes he serves, work precisely to expose such glorious disguises.

—Barbara Hodgdon, *The End Crowns All: Closure and Contradiction in Shakespeare's History* (Princeton, NJ: Princeton Univ, Press, 1991), pp. 155–156.

[Bernard J. Paris, a professor of English at the University of Florida, has written several books, including *Character and Conflict in Jane Austen's Novels* (1978), *Bargains with Fate: Psychological Crises and Conflicts in Shakespeare and His Plays* (1991), and *Character as a Subversive Force in Shakespeare* (1991), from which the following extract is taken. Here, Paris maintains that Shakespeare makes it clear in *Henry IV, Part One,* that King Henry is wrong in his denigration of Hal and his vaunting of Hotspur.]

In *1 Henry IV*, Hal's detractors are King Henry and Hotspur. In the opening scene Henry envies Northumberland for having "A son who is the theme of honour's tongue," while "riot and dishonour stain the brow / Of my young Harry"; and he wishes that Hotspur were his son instead of Henry. When Hal returns to court, the King attacks him for his "inordinate and low desires," accuses him of "vassal fear" and "Base inclination," and compares him unfavorably to Hotspur, who "hath more worthy interest to the state / Than thou, the shadow of succession" (3.2). Hotspur refers to him contemptuously as the "madcap Prince of Wales" (4.1) whom he "would have poisoned with a pot of ale" were it not for the fact that "his father loves him not / And would be glad he met with some mischance" (1.3). The play as a whole moves toward the battle of Shrewsbury where Hal proves both his loyalty and prowess, defeats one of his detractors, converts the other, and demonstrates his worthiness of the throne.

From the beginning, however, Shakespeare is at pains to let us know that Henry is wrong in his judgment of Hal's character and of his worth in relation to Hotspur. Immediately after the King's complaints about Hal, we see Hal with Falstaff, who is proposing that thievery be countenanced and gallows removed when Hal becomes king. The issue, says (C. L.) Barber, is whether "the interregnum of a Lord of Misrule, delightful in its moment, might develop into the anarchic reign of a favorite dominating a dissolute king." When Hal responds to Falstaff's "Do not thou, when thou art king, hang a thief" by saying that Falstaff shall "have the hanging of the thieves" (1.2), he is making it clear that he will not be a dissolute king. Unlike the Prince in *The Famous Victories of Henry the Fifth,* Hal is not himself a criminal. He refuses to participate in the Gadshill affair ("Who, I rob? I a thief? Not I, by my faith"), wavers a moment under pressure from Falstaff ("Well, then, once in my days I'll be a madcap"), then determines to "tarry at home" (1.2). He goes along only after Poins proposes that the two of them rob the thieves rather than the travelers, and he arranges to have the booty returned.

Shakespeare's presentation of Hal in the second scene of the play is a response to Harry's complaints in the first. He raises the question through Falstaff's speeches of whether Hal will be a lawless king and immediately provides us with evidence that he will not. In case we have missed the point, Hal's soliloquy should leave no doubt. What this speech tells us about Hal's character is a matter of considerable controversy, but it seems fairly clear that it is an important rhetorical device. It lets us know that Hal is aware of the deficiencies of his companions and means to remain with them for only a limited period of time, that he will "throw off" his "loose behaviour" when the right moment arrives, and that he will live up to the demands of his role and the values of his community. The soliloquy generates a great deal of dramatic irony, since it gives us more information about Hal than is possessed by the characters in the play and makes us aware of the inappropriateness of their expectations and anxieties. It creates expectations in the audience that are then fulfilled by the ensuing action, partially in part 1 and completely in part 2. The expectation is not for reformation, but for vindication. We know that Henry and Hotspur are wrong about Hal, and we await their acknowledgement of his worth. We know that his vindication will seem like a reformation to other people, but we also know that Hal will not change in any fundamental way. Rather, he will appear to be what he really is; he will display his virtues at last.

As the play progresses, Shakespeare employs other foreshadowing devices that contribute to the rhetoric of vindication. Hal assures Falstaff that he is not afraid of the approaching confrontation with Douglas and Percy (2.4); he lets Falstaff know, only half in jest, that he will banish him (2.4); he promises his father that he "shall here-after . . . / Be more [him]self" (3.2); and he predicts his battlefield triumphs, which will win him all the glory Percy has accumulated and will wash away his shame. Since the action confirms all that Hal says, we are left with the impression that he can do whatever he wishes; he is not torn between virtue and vice, nobility and degeneracy, but is simply choosing when to display his true self. His vindication, both in this play and the next, is foreshadowed also by Vernon's praise, which, coming from an adversary, carries much weight: "England did never owe so sweet a hope, / So much misconstrued in his wantonness" (5.3). There is a similar speech by Warwick in part 2, in which he tells Henry that his son "but studies his companions," whom he will "cast off" in "the perfectness of time" (4.4). His "memory" of them will help to form his judgment, thus "turning past evils to advantages." Both of these speeches present Hal not as a dissolute young man who will reform, but as a noble young man who has been "misconstrued," and the audience knows that they are right before the action proves them to be so.

In *1 Henry IV*, the primary contrast is between Prince Hal and Hotspur, to whom the King twice compares his son, to Hal's great disadvantage. Part of Shakespeare's rhetoric of vindication is to develop the comparison dramatically in such a way as to show Hal to be the better man, and this from the start. The King is mistaken not only about Hal, but also about Hotspur, who does embody certain martial virtues in which Hal is, for the moment, deficient, but who also embodies the defects of those virtues, and who behaves self-destructively as a result. Whereas Shakespeare consistently justifies Hal, he consistently satirizes Hotspur, who lacks all balance and self-control.

—Bernard J. Paris, *Character as a Subversive Force in Shakespeare: The History and Roman Plays* (Rutherford, NJ: Fairleigh Dickinson Univ. Press, 1991), pp. 74–76.

Plot Summary of
Henry IV, Part 2

Lord Bardolph wakes Northumberland with the "good tidings" that Prince Harry is dead and that Falstaff is Prince Hal's prisoner (**Act I**, scene 1). Northumberland's grief over the death of his son strengthens his resolve against the Lancasters: "In poison there is physic, and these news, / Having been well, that would have made me sick, / Being sick, have in some measure made me well: /. . . Now bind my brows with iron; and approach / The ragged'st hour that time and spite dare bring / To frown upon the enraged Northumberland! / Let heaven kiss earth! now let not Nature's hand / Keep the wild flood confin'd! let order die!" Travers and Morton, Northumberland's retainers, arrive with more details of the battle at Shrewsbury. Northumberland vows to extend the rebellion against the king; Morton reminds him that their cause had been to avenge the death of Richard II (and to gain the throne for Mortimer, the legitimate heir).

Scene 2 opens upon Sir John Falstaff with his page. In this comic scene Falstaff verbally parries with the Lord Chief Justice, whom he passes on a London street. The Chief Justice accuses Falstaff of having "misled the youthful prince," and that his "day's service at [the battle at] Shrewsbury hath a little gilded over [his] night's exploit on Gadshill" (see *1 Henry IV, II.2*). Falstaff informs him that he will join Lord John of Lancaster in the fight against the Archbishop of York and the Earl of Northumberland. The Justice is impressed and wishes him well. Falstaff asks, "Will your lordship lend me a thousand pound to furnish me forth?" He, of course, refuses and leaves. Falstaff remarks to his page, "I can get no remedy against this consumption of the purse; borrowing only lingers it out, but the disease is incurable." He sends him with letters to Lord Lancaster, "the Prince," the Earl of Westmoreland, and "to old Mistress Ursula, whom I have weekly sworn to marry since I perceiv'd the first white hair of my chin."

In scene 3, the Archbishop of York, Lord Mowbray, Lord Hastings, and Lord Bardolph meet to plan the next battle in their rebellion against King Henry. Bardolph remarks the foolishness of Hotspur who had "lin'd himself with hope, / Eating the air on promise of supply, / Flattering himself in project of a power / Much smaller than the smallest of his thoughts: / And so with great imagination, / Proper to madmen, led his powers to death, / And winking, leap'd into destruction." The quality of Hotspur's hope is very like the problem they now face that "[l]ike one that draws the model of an house / Beyond his power to build it," they and their allies lack the unity necessary to ensure victory. York tells them that "[t]he commonwealth is sick of their own choice" and that they may count on the support of the people in their rebellion against the crown.

In London, in the street in front of a tavern (**Act II**, scene 1), Fang and Snare discuss with the tavern hostess, Mistress Quickly, the lawsuit they intend to file against Falstaff, who owes her a debt. She complains that "[a] hundred mark is a long [debt] for a poor lone woman to bear, and I have borne, and borne, and borne, and have been fubb'd off, and fubb'd off, and fubb'd off, from this day to that day, that it is a shame to be thought on." Falstaff arrives with his page, and the ensuing ruckus attracts the attention of the Lord Chief Justice and his men. The Justice determines that Falstaff has "practic'd upon the easy-yielding spirit of this woman, and made her serve [his] uses both in purse and in person." He advises Falstaff to pay his debt on both accounts. Master Gower arrives with a message that the King and Harry, Prince of Wales, will arrive soon at the tavern. The Prince and Poins arrive at the tavern in scene 2. Prince Hal seems to have reversed his movement toward behavior more befitting a future king that he displayed at the end of Part 1. The comic underplot of Falstaff's outrageous doings continues to engage the prince.

In scene 3 the widowed Lady Percy begs her father-in-law "for God's sake, go not to these wars!" She suggests that he is more committed in his support of the Archbishop's forces than he was in his support of his own son: "Never, O never, do [Hotspur's] ghost the wrong / To hold your honor more precise and nice / With others than with him." The point is well taken, but Northumberland sees no choice: "I must go and meet with danger there, / Or it will seek me in another place, / And find me worse provided," he replies.

At the Boar's Head Tavern with Falstaff (scene 4), in bawdy revelry with Doll Tearsheet, Mistress Quickly, Bardolph and his page, Ancient Pistol, and Poins, Prince Hal receives a message that "a dozen captains, / Bare-headed, sweating, knocking at the taverns, / [Are] asking every one for Sir John Falstaff." Anticipating a certain "tempest and commotion," Prince Hal and Poins leave.

In **Act III**, scene 1, the king, in the palace at Westminster, sends his page to the earls of Surrey and of Warwick with letters and a command that they appear that night. He cannot sleep for worry over the rebellion and of perils both past and likely to come. "Uneasy lies the head that wears a crown," he muses to himself. Warwick, Surrey, and Blunt arrive and do their best to reassure the king that their cause has always been just and that rumors of the rebellion's strength are exaggerated. Warwick advises, "Your Majesty hath been this fortnight ill; / And these unseason'd hours perforce must add / Unto hour sickness." The king replies, "I will take your counsel: / And were these inward wars once out of hand, / We would, dear lords, unto the Holy Land." He never makes the pilgrimage, although he will die in the Jerusalem Chamber of Westminster Abbey (Act IV, scene 5).

Act III, scene 2 opens upon a meeting of unsavory characters before Justice Shallow's house in Gloucestershire. Their gossip is interrupted by the arrival of Falstaff, who joins the conversation. Summoned to the army for the repression of the rebellion and recruiting support for the king, he falls in with Justices Shallow and Silence and extracts money from Shallow.

Prince Harry sits at his father's deathbed in **Act IV**, scene 5. Harry notices the soundness of the king's sleep and reveals the impatience that is companion to his ambition: "This sleep is sound indeed; this is a sleep / That from this golden rigol [circle, i.e. the crown] hath divorced / So many English kings. / . . . My due from thee is this imperial crown, / Which, as immediate from thy place and blood, / Derives itself to me." He puts on the crown and exits. The king awakes and cries out for Warwick, Gloucester, and Clarence, telling them to "[G]o, seek him out. / Is he so hasty that he doth suppose / My sleep my death?" Warwick returns with the prince and Henry bitterly upbraids him. Prince Hal assures him that he has only respect for his father's power. Henry recalls the devious acts by which he gained the throne and warns Hal that he may need to guard against civil unrest by pursuing "foreign quarrels," foreshadowing the campaign against France depicted in *Henry V.* Father and son are reconciled before Henry IV dies.

Falstaff comes to greet his old friend, the newly crowned King Henry V (**Act V**, scene 5). Hal rejects him. "I know thee not, old man. Fall to thy prayers; / . . . Presume not I am the thing I was; / For God doth know, so shall the world perceive, / That I have turn'd away my former self." He sends Falstaff away but allows him "competence of life." Prophesying the future—and Shakespeare's next play—Sir John of Lancaster remarks, "I will lay odds that, ere this year expire, / We bear our civil swords and native fire / As far as France." ❀

List of Characters in
Henry IV, Part 2

King Henry IV, a careworn ruler, sleepless with the burdens of his office, candidly assesses his career as he prepares to die. On his deathbed he warns his son against the continued influence of Falstaff: "For the Fift Harry from curb'd license plucks / The muzzle of restraint, and the wild dog / Shall flesh his tooth on every innocent." But Hal has already realized the danger.

Prince Henry, or Hal (afterward crowned **King Henry V**) is transformed over the course of the play from a madcap and irresponsible prince into a wise and able king, an Elizabethan version of the story of the prodigal son. His speech moves from prose to verse, from disgrace to honor as he embodies more kingly virtues.

Sir John Falstaff is an authentic triumph of literary imagination. He is a dazzling intellect and a genius of rhetoric, as well as a liar, glutton, lecher, and thief. His sharp wit and novel perspectives work with his verbal skill to shape a complex comic vision. But, by his disrespect for the moral, social, and political structures that inhibit most of us and with his easy freedom, he represents a very real danger to Hal. He is a test to Hal's preparation to assume the crown. Hal finally rejects him.

Prince John of Lancaster; Humphrey, duke of Gloucester; and **Thomas, duke of Clarence** are sons of Henry IV; brothers of Henry V.

Earl of Northumberland, Archbishop of York, Lords Mowbray, Hastings, and **Bardolph** are members of the rebellion against Henry IV.

Earls of Warwick, Westmoreland, and Surrey, Sir Walter Blunt, and **Lord Chief Justice** are members of the King Henry IV's retinue.

Poins, Bardolph, Pistol, and **Doll Tearsheet** are tavern habituees and humorists.

Hostess Quickly runs the Boar's Head Tavern, Eastcheap, London.

Shallow and **Silence** are country justices.

Fang and **Snare** are sergeants in the king's service. ❁

Critical Views on
Henry IV, Part 2

SIGURD BURCKHARDT ON THE PLAY'S OVERTURNING
OF THE "TUDOR MYTH" OF HISTORY

[Sigurd Burckhardt (1916–1966) is author of *Shakespearean Meanings* and *The Drama of Language: Essays on Goethe and Kleist.* In this excerpt, Burckhardt argues that the "Tudor myth" of history, the belief that a cosmic order is reasserted after periods of chaos and civil strife, is challenged in the play as Prince Hal "moves toward the accession and 'victorious acts' of a king whose title is almost non-lineal, one short link removed from the breach."]

Two things about *2 Henry IV* are clear: it is designed to culminate in Hal's accession; and it disappoints our expectation (aroused by the play itself) of reaching that point through the "plain shock and even play of battle." To gauge our disappointment, we need only imagine the following: that Shakespeare had written *Henry IV* in one part, climaxing in the battle of Shrewsbury; that the king had died right after the battle, so that Hal's accession would have followed immediately upon his battlefield triumph; and that Hal had at that point exposed Falstaff's cowardice and lies, making them the occasion of rejecting him and signifying his own resolution to be a just and sober as well as valiant king. The distortion and telescoping of historical facts would have been no worse than what Shakespeare permits himself elsewhere; and I am by no means the first to suggest that such a way of managing the story would have been dramatically much more satisfying than the two-part arrangement Shakespeare chose.

In fact, up to the point of his seizing the crown, it appears that Hal is quite deliberately being kept *out of* [Part II]. Of the only two scenes he is given prior to that point, the second (II, iv) is almost wholly dominated by Falstaff and his gentlewomen; the Prince's puny jest is just sufficient—and is *meant*—to remind us of the lost glories of the corresponding scene in Part I (II, iv.).

Clearly the theory that in Part II Hal proves himself just (as in Part I he proved himself valorous), while it has a certain *a priori* plausibility, is sadly lacking in dramatic substance. But just as clearly the play is *about* Hal and culminates in his accession. What, then, is Hal's role; what does he *do*, except remind us that he is doing nothing? The answer is simple: prior to his accession, Hal has one role only—that of heir, of *successor*.

Our seeing Hal as stripped of all roles except that of successor helps us account for several oddities. It accounts for the omission of the scene in which Hal strikes the Chief Justice; it accounts for his non-appearance at court and his non-participation in the affairs of the realm.

It would seem that we need to think carefully about the problem of *succession*. What is it? What does it rest on? What does it entail?

It has been shown that the governing theme of the history plays, derived by Shakespeare from Hall's *Union of the Noble and Illustre Famelies of Lancastre and Yorke,* is that of the disturbed succession. But I shall argue that for Shakespeare the disturbance was vastly more radical and encompassing than we have realized; that it involved not merely England but the entire moral universe; and, most importantly, that its consequences were *irreversible.* To put it somewhat provocatively: in the deposition of Richard II Shakespeare discovered the decomposition of a world picture; we are wrong in assuming that his world picture was still that of Hall and Tudor doctrine.

At first glance it seems obvious that Shakespeare's histories recognize only one mode of succession as truly legitimate: Primogeniture. Other modes—particularly succession by combat, as described in Frazer's *Golden Bough*—seem clearly illegitimate; indeed they are not alternate modes so much as lapses into chaos. (Succession by popular election can readily be interpreted as a variant of succession by combat.) All the same it would be very easy for an anthropological critic to read the history plays as recording a series of successions by combat, in which kings who are lacking in potency are supplanted (and usually killed) by others who prove their right to the title by their ability to seize it. Indeed, if this critic were rigorously descriptive and inferred the law of succession in the histories strictly from the actual events, he could not possibly arrive at the law of primogeniture. Richard II to Henry IV, Henry VI to Edward IV, Edward V to Richard III, Richard III to Henry VII—by the combat mode this succession is close to "unbroken," certainly much less broken than under the mode of primogeniture. Depending on the model we choose, the same sequence will appear as either reasonably orderly or disastrously chaotic.

Of course, if we chose the combat model we would completely pervert the meaning of Hall and other Tudor historians and do at least some violence to Shakespeare's. Still I cannot help asking: how much violence? Tudor political theorists and propagandists were always ready to quote St. Paul to the effect that all power is from God, whence it followed that the subject owed obedience, as a matter of religious duty, to the *de facto* ruler. It does not take much thought to discover that this argument implies a combat model of succession; a little more thought may even lead to the suspicion that there is a remarkably close, perhaps necessary, connection between this model and a divinely ruled universe. However that may be, the Tudors were not foolhardy enough to rest their title on the Pauline principle alone; a great deal of effort and ingenuity was expended in proving that the title was (primogenitively) legitimate. Tudor propaganda left little to chance; it worked both sides of the royal road. The title was legitimate beyond question; and even if it was not, it still was. Heads the king won, tails the doubting subject lost—his head most likely if he was rash enough to ask for the toss.

I do not mean that the deception was conscious; the apologists of the Tudor establishment were, I expect, all honorable men, and in any case there is hardly a limit to the inconsistencies men manage sincerely to believe where their needs and vital interests are at stake. . . . Under these circumstances it was natural that even thoughtful men should, as occasions demanded, feel quite untroubled about applying one or the other of these concepts of legitimacy, or even both simultaneously, without realizing that they entailed mutually inconsistent world pictures. But I believe that Shakespeare—who was a more than ordinarily thoughtful man—did see the inconsistency.

I am aware that my ideas on the meaning of "succession" must seem wholly un-Shakespearean in spirit. Few things are as firmly established as that the history plays adopt and follow the great scheme of Tudor history. Far from being caused by the law of primogeniture, England's troubles from Richard II to Henry VII were both the result of and the punishment for the *breach* of that law. (We note in passing how in this account the two models—causal and juridical—are mixed.) Of all the lessons to be learned from history, that is the one most insistently pointed by Hall, as well as by many of Shakespeare's characters. Even Henry V recites it when he implores God's help in the night before Agincourt.

The argument, I grant, looks strong; all the same I find it less and less tenable. What does the orthodox scheme entail? Most importantly it entails the belief that in the long run, if not in the short, the movement of history is *restorative*. The cosmic order has been disturbed by man; after a while, and often at great cost to man, it reasserts itself. The scheme of Hall's *Union* satisfies this assumption perfectly; it traces English history from the fatal breach to the happy restoration. But Shakespeare's histories do *not* satisfy it; his second tetralogy ends in the middle of the story, with the usurper Henry V at the high tide of glory and good fortune.

The structure of the second tetralogy . . . is *not* restorative. It moves toward the accession and "victorious acts" of a king whose title is almost non-lineal, one short link removed from the breach. This king is not sent by God as a redeemer; we observe him grooming himself for his role with the cool calculations of Richard III (though of course by wholly different means). I think we need to be cautious about calling Henry V Shakespeare's "ideal king"; but to a remarkable degree he is *self-made*. His title is legitimized largely by his self-nurtured qualities and by his achievements; when God "crowns" him with victory, that legitimation is *ex post facto*.

We misread the second tetralogy if we think of it as "really" the first. The chronology that counts is not that of English history but that of Shakespeare's plays—which is to say, of his development as a dramatist. There is no evidence for considering the second tetralogy a revision of some lost plays; but there are some very good reasons for considering it as a revision of the first tetralogy—as a revision dictated by the discovery that restoration is a false ideal. Time, like a line, moves in one direction only; and drama, especially historical drama, is action in time.

—Sigurd Burckhardt, "'Swoll'n with Some Other Grief': Shakespeare's Prince Hal Trilogy," in his *Shakespearean Meanings* (Princeton, NJ: Princeton Univ. Press, 1968), pp. 144–205. Reprinted in *Shakespearean Criticism* 1. Laurie Lanzen Harris, ed. (Detroit: Gale, 1984): pp. 422–423.]

James Winny on the Autonomy of Parts 1 and 2

[In this excerpt, Winny argues for the relative autonomy of Parts 1 and 2 of *Henry IV*. He also regards Shakespeare's English histories as unified only in the common exploration of the theme of self-deception, specifically with respect to the kings. He thus contradicts Schlegel and Tillyard, both of whom identify Shakespeare's English histories as a unified "epic" of either eight or ten plays.]

Belief that the history-plays act out the moral argument of the Homilies has encouraged an assumption that eight of the plays form tetralogies, to be read as a continuous work showing the evil consequences of deposing Richard II, which were to trouble England for the next eighty years. This view of the Histories is open to several objections. The most obvious is that their order of composition suggests no such purpose. Had Shakespeare intended from the outset to make the crime of deposing a lawful king responsible for all the disorder and havoc which the two tetralogies depict, he would hardly have chosen to begin his series with *Henry VI*, historically the midpoint of the whole timespan which his plays cover. . . . It is more reasonable to suppose that if the Histories contain some collective meaning, it is compatible with their order of composition.

[In all of the histories] the efforts of a king to impose his authority upon an unruly kingdom, or to resist the challenge of open rebellion, is a matter of first account. The persistence of this subject, from *Henry VI* onwards, has been the main support of interpretations based upon the political morality of the Homilies, and of the argument that the two tetralogies show the consequences of lifting hands against God's deputy. If, instead, we assume that Shakespeare used the matter of the English chronicles for an essentially imaginative purpose, the repeated—and generally unsuccessful—attempts of a king to assert his authority over rebellious subjects take on a very different appearance. It now becomes a point of imaginative significance that none of the six kings in these eight plays enjoys an undisputed title to the crown, and must fight to retain it. The first of Shakespeare's sovereigns, 'in infant bands crowned king', is the weakest and least effectual in resisting the challenge to his title and possession; the last the strongest and most assured of his legiti-macy. This development running through the Histories, by which the king acquires an increasing force of authority, shows why it must be mistaken to treat the series as though it were intended to begin with the deposition of Richard and to end with the accession of Henry Tudor. The historical order of the six reigns is not relevant to Shakespeare's imaginative purpose: the chronological order of the plays is. ⟨...⟩

In many important respects Hal presents ... an antithesis to Boling-broke so pointed that his dramatic character seems largely determined by the terms of this inverted relationship. If Falstaff is comic shadow to Bolingbroke, the Prince is his reverse image, duplicating his father's habits in the opposite moral sense, by presenting virtue in the guise of vice. Where Hal's behaviour is not psychologically accountable we may look for its explanation in the imaginative design which obliges him to act as though in deliberate contrast to Bolingbroke, taking a path which tacitly dissociates him from all that his father represents.

Bolingbroke, Hotspur and the Prince have more in common than the name Harry, which helps to suggest an obscure relationship between all three. Each has adopted a moral disguise, the two imposters passing themselves off as authentic, and the true prince deliberately bringing his genuineness into doubt. Bolingbroke grudg-ingly acknowledges his heir, but envies Northumberland his Harry, and wishes their sons might be exchanged; not appreciating that the traitor Harry Hotspur might fittingly regard him as father of his law-less enterprise, and that Hal is indeed a stranger to him except in blood. Their likeness of moral character makes it appropriate that the King should wish to recognise Hotspur as heir, and that Hotspur should act the part of prodigal son to this father-figure; but Hal has imperative reasons for insisting upon his legitimacy, and for offering positive proof of the identity which Hotspur is trying to steal from him. 'I will redeem all this on Percy's head,' he promises Bolingbroke;

> And in the closing of some glorious day
> Be bold to tell you that I am your son,
> When I will wear a garment all of blood,
> And stain my favours in a bloody mask,
> Which, washed away, shall scour my shame with it.
> [*1 Henry IV,* III.ii.133–37].

Hal's descent to the murky world of the taverns does not prepare him for kingship. It represents the adoption of a moral attitude exactly opposite to the position taken up by Bolingbroke and Hotspur in common, a mask of dishonour assumed as though in protest against the spurious nobility of both. The audience is invited to recognise the Prince as the moral antithesis of Bolingbroke, and to find assurance in Hal's behaviour that the next king will reverse all the practices by which Bolingbroke has corrupted law and truth. The killing of Hotspur, an image of the prince whom Bol-ingbroke wishes his son to be, is an earnest of Hal's ultimate intention.

The purpose which he discloses at his accession admits more than his own past wildness. 'The tide of blood in me,' he tells the Lord Chief Justice,

> Hath proudly flowed in vanity till now;
> Now doth it turn and ebb back to the sea,
> Where it shall mingle with the state of floods,
> And flow henceforth in formal majesty.
>
> [*2 Henry IV*, V.ii.129–33]

The tide withdrawing from inland creeks to the open sea represents the Prince who has abandoned Eastcheap for ever, but much more the final dissociation of the blood-royal from the dishonours which Bolingbroke rather than Hal has brought upon it. Although Hal's moral reformation involves some calculated pretence, it is not simply hypocritical. The change of character which he appears to undergo is a true index of the transformation worked upon the king's office and person as Hal restores dignity to both. By concealing his nobility under the moment of his accession, he is able to show in himself how completely sovereignty is to renounce its long association with crime. A prince who had not disguised his respect for law would be incapable of making this deeply symbolic gesture, whose purpose is not to illuminate Hal's character but to round off the imaginative design of the play in a strong dramatic image.

This reinstating of justice [Hal's reappointment of the Lord Chief Justice] after the confusions of Bolingbroke's imposture restores the positive standards which the old king's falseness has thrown into question. By presenting his actual nobility as dishonour, Hal has made himself a stranger to the inverted moral values upheld by Bolingbroke, and shown his critical discrimination between the substance and form of truth; while the King, through habitual counterfeiting, has lost his power of distinguishing between the false and the authentic. The new king now brings his discrimination to bear upon the ambiguous appearances which have checked and harassed the process of law during the reign of a usurper, and chooses without hesitation between the real and the spurious figures of justice which claim the office. In making this disclosure of his true self, Hal also restores the image of sovereignty defaced by his father, whose dissimulating of royalty set an example of doubling and equivocation throughout his kingdom. With the passing of old Double and the public rejection of the father-figure in whom Bolingbroke's vices are impudently parodied, the moral inversions of the reign are brought to an end. The prodigal father is succeeded by a just son; and the royal estate is inherited by an heir whose personal truth, in its various senses, is made imaginatively equivalent with an unchallengeable right to the name of king.

—James Winny, "Introduction" and "The Royal Counterfeit," in his *The Player King: A Theme of Shakespeare's Histories* (London: Chatto & Windus, 1968), pp. 9–47, 86–167. Reprinted in *Shakespearean Criticism* 1. Laurie Lanzen Harris, ed. (Detroit: Gale, 1984): pp. 426–427.

[In this excerpt, Bergeron analyzes how Shakespeare wrestles
with Falstaff's question, "Is not the truth the truth?" and, in the
process, how he challenges the purposes of history in the confrontation of narrative history and narrative fiction in *Part 2*.]

In the tavern scene in *1 Henry IV,* Falstaff asks somewhat incredulously:
"Is not the truth the truth?" Shakespeare explores the province of history by wrestling with Falstaff's question, raising doubts about the very
purpose of history that some critics have assumed define the history
play. Nowhere is the evidence of making history more apparent than in
2 Henry IV. In Act IV the Archbishop of York says of King Henry: he
will "keep no tell-tale to his memory / That may repeat and *history* his
loss / To new remembrance" (IV.i.202–204). Shakespeare uses "history"
as a verb only this one time in the entire canon. This special focus on
the word "history" corresponds to an unusually rich concern for the
issues of history in 2 *Henry IV,* a self-consciousness about history that I
do not perceive in the earlier English history plays. ⟨ . . . ⟩

Constructing history underscores its fictional quality. Louis O. Mink
writes: "narrative form in history, as in fiction, is an artifice, the product
of individual imagination." Into the debate among contemporary historians about the function of narrative in historical writing—indeed, the
occasional blurring of history and fiction—Shakespeare had already
stepped several centuries earlier by means of his dramatic fiction. In
fact, Shakespeare regularly "makes" history, especially in the early years
of his dramatic career. He was, of course, not alone. The final two
decades of the sixteenth century witnessed an outpouring of historical
drama: plays by Marlowe, Peele, anonymous dramatists, and others.
The Famous Victories of Henry V, for example, lies as a probable source
behind Shakespeare's *Henry IV* plays; his *Richard II* has close affinities
with Marlowe's *Edward II.* One can multiply the examples of historical
drama and Shakespeare's participation in this development as the century closes. Ribner says that a history play is "an adaptation of drama to
the purposes of history," but therein lies the interpretive problem.

The ordered, providential concept of history, epitomized in Tillyard's
seminal study of the history plays and accepted by Ribner, has given way
to a recognition that Shakespeare exhibits a sophisticated and at times
problematic understanding of the nature of history. David Quint has
argued that in "Shakespeare's poetic treatment, history ceases to be the
didactic instrument of classical humanism and becomes instead an
occasion for historicist self-reflection." Graham Holderness takes the
matter farther when he writes: "Shakespeare's historical plays are not
just *reflections* of a cultural debate: they are *interventions* in that debate,
contributions to the historiographical effort to reconstruct the past and
discover the methods and principles of that reconstruction." Writing
itself, as Michel de Certeau and others have noted, produces history.

Certeau suggests that writing is an archive that makes possible the creation of a stable history. Anyone familiar with Shakespeare's use of his sources in the history plays knows how the dramatist reshapes history to suit artistic purposes.

This shaping of history is especially characteristic of *2 Henry IV*. If, for example, we think of the three parts of *Henry VI* and *Richard III*, we do not find there a grappling with historical problems on the magnitude of *2 Henry IV*; these plays seem more a relatively straight-forward chronicle of events. *Edward II, The Famous Victories*, and *The Life and Death of Jack Straw* all focus on historical action without, I think, an understanding of the problematic nature of history itself. Even in Shakespeare's second tetralogy, *2 Henry IV* stands out because it is more self-aware of its literary history. By this I mean that it pays relatively more attention to its indebtedness to the drama that has preceded it. It is, for example, the only one of the Henriad plays that quotes directly from its predecessor—in this case, *Richard II*. In a word, *2 Henry IV* looks back with a historical perspective unlike the other plays of its group, including *Henry V*, which takes little notice of its precursors: witness the *report* of Falstaff's death, a sign of this play's distance from the others. ⟨ . . . ⟩

Falstaff wanders between narrative truth and narrative fiction, between Shakespeare's rendering of national history and his creative license. Falstaff is historical because he exists in Shakespeare's literary history, clearly a fictional adjunct in the midst of political and military history. I argue that the dramatist also intends an identification between Falstaff and Rumour, a point also made by Porter and Abrams. The Hostess says of Falstaff: "he's an infinitive thing upon my score" (II.i.23). Though she presumably means "infinite," the idea of Falstaff as "infinitive" appeals. Rumour in the Induction makes clear its infinitive: "My office is / To noise abroad" (lines 28–29). Similarly, Falstaff noises abroad all kinds of half-truths or lies. His infinitive? "To lie" or "to counterfeit," to cite his term from *1 Henry IV*. He has, for example, promised to marry Hostess Quickly, but clearly does not intend to do that. As the Chief Justice notes, Falstaff has the "manner of wrenching the true cause the false way" (II.i.108–109). Falstaff claims later: "I have a whole school of tongues in this belly of mine" (IV.iii.18). This image deliberately recalls Rumour, "*painted full of tongues.*" It is tempting to imagine Falstaff's costume as containing pictures of tongues. Such loose tongues, untroubled by constraints of truth, noise abroad, slander, and deceive. Rumour offers a link to Falstaff: "what need I thus / My well-known body to anatomize" (Induction 20–21). The best-known body would likely be Falstaff's. The emphasis on Falstaff's *body* underscores the carnivalesque quality of his character. His irreverent, threatening, unruly, ludicrous, and possibly subversive qualities derive in part from carnival. In Rumour and Falstaff Shakespeare epitomizes the difficulty of establishing credible history.

The Chief Justice says to Falstaff: "You follow the young Prince up and down, like his ill angel" (I.ii.162–63)—another variation of Rumour. As such, Falstaff has "misled the youthful Prince" (line 143); to which Falstaff retorts: "The young Prince hath misled me. I am the fellow with the great belly, and he my dog." The Justice also likens Falstaff to a candle, "the better part burnt out" (lines 155–56). But Falstaff's presumed valorous past mitigates these charges: "Your day's service at Shrewsbury hath a little gilded over your night's exploit on Gad's Hill" (lines 147–48), says the Justice. One wonders exactly what "service" at Shrewsbury the Justice recalls; he has apparently accepted the story of Falstaff's slaying of Hotspur. If so, this scene, like the play's first, illustrates the process of constructing history—the selective use of detail, the synecdoche of history. With Falstaff involved, one always encounters difficulties. Despite his size, he functions like a moving target, impossible to pin down and possessing elusive, ahistorical qualities: a fiction that threatens the making of history.

Having just learned about the "history in all men's lives" in III.i, we hear a different kind of history in III.ii: that of Justices Shallow and Silence, who focus not only on their past experiences but also on the issue of death. Shallow says: "Death, as the Psalmist saith, is certain to all, all shall die" (lines 36–37). Here in another key the dramatist through his characters confronts death as a constituent part of history, as he had in Lady Percy's appearance in II.iii. With Shallow's question, "O, Sir John, do you remember since we lay all night in the Windmill in Saint George's Field?" (lines 189–90), Falstaff enters their historical recollection, noting that they have indeed "heard the chimes at midnight" (line 209). Even "ahistory" may proceed by presumed memory. The synecdochic remembrance nevertheless must meet another test: credibility. Falstaff, the incarnation of Rumour, challenges the validity of the stories that he has heard, not unlike Northumberland's sifting of evidence in the play's first scene. Falstaff complains: "Lord, Lord, how subject we old men are to this vice of lying! This same starved justice hath done nothing but prate to me of the wilderness of his youth, . . . and every third word a lie" (lines 296–301).

Just as Westmoreland undermines Mowbray's account of his father's tournament encounter with Bolingbroke (IV.i.), so Falstaff reinterprets the shallow and silent history of these minor justices. Justice Shallow's references to "John a Gaunt" particularly gall Falstaff: "I'll be sworn a [he] ne'er saw him [Gaunt] but once in the tiltyard, and then he burst his head for crowding among the marshal's men" (lines 316–18). With delicious historical irony, Falstaff then says: "I saw it and told John a Gaunt he beat his own name" (lines 318–19). In this special moment Shakespeare combines in the ahistorical Falstaff national and literary history. Falstaff seems to be part of national history but is indeed credible only in Shakespeare's own artistic work. And yet in an irony that doubles back on itself, the ahistorical character challenges the historical veracity of other ahistorical characters who have invoked a memory of their involvement with a historically great figure, John of Gaunt.

This same Falstaff captures one of the rebels, Coleville of the Dale, in IV.iii as his fictional world intersects with Prince John's exploits. When chided for his tardiness in arriving at the battle, Falstaff replies: "Do you think me a swallow, an arrow, or a bullet?" (lines 32–33). An invisible bullet, Falstaff cannot be found in history's chronicles. But for his valorous "conquest" of Coleville, Falstaff insists that it should "be booked with the rest of this day's deeds" (lines 45–46)—or perhaps a ballad or picture to capture the moment before it speeds away from memory. With such recordations of his deeds Falstaff conceives an image of himself: "I in the clear sky of fame o'er shine you as much as the full moon doth the cinders of the element" (lines 50–52). In the clear sky of fame resides Rumour/Falstaff. The only "booking" that Falstaff receives is Shakespeare's play. Of course the news of Prince Hal's accession to the throne leads Pistol to assert to Falstaff: "thou art now one of the greatest men in this realm" (V.iii.85–86). Caught up in the excitement, Falstaff claims: "I am Fortune's steward!" (lines 126–27). The desire to be written down in historical chronicles, to shine in Fame's clear sky, and to serve as Fortune's steward reinforces Falstaff's vainglorious concept of himself. History will finally puncture this illusion and expel "ahistory."

When Prince Hal becomes Henry V in the play's last act, the dramatist returns to the question of rumor with which the play began. The new king makes a speech of reconciliation to the Chief Justice and to his brothers. He says:

> My father is gone wild into his grave,
> For in his tomb lie my affections;
> And with his spirits sadly I survive
> To mock the expectation of the world,
> To frustrate prophecies, and to raze out
> Rotten opinion, who hath writ me down
> After my seeming.
>
> (V.ii.123–29)

The history of Prince Hal, written down after his seeming, contains rotten opinion and rumor to which his new life as king will give the lie. As Abrams notes, in one sense Rumour is Hal's adversary. His living history will supplant and subvert the record, establishing a truth not subject to rumor. Like the carnivalesque Falstaff, Prince Hal will mock expectations, rendering suspect historical prophecies about himself. Like Falstaff, the new king will mock conventional ideas about history; instead, he will construct a new history by erasing what has already been written about him. Overthrowing history is part of the process of making history. The new king readies himself to confront Falstaff in a final battle of competing histories.

—David M. Bergeron, "Shakespeare Makes History: *2 Henry IV*," in *Studies in English Literature 1500–1900* 31, no. 2 (Spring 1991): 231–245. Reprinted in *Shakespearean Criticism* 30. Marie Lazzari, ed. (Detroit: Gale, 1991): pp. 143–144, 148–149.

[In this excerpt, Weiss maintains that through the character of
Prince Hal, Shakespeare constructs a play that is as accomplished as a comedy as it is a history.]

Henry IV ⟨ . . . ⟩ is as free a play, as expansive, complex, and buoyantly
inclusive, as any Shakespeare ever wrote. Here he gives his time, now
of all humours, full voice. In *Richard II*, celebrating the climax and
death of English Medievalism, Shakespeare, like Richard himself,
compressed his powers in one splendid if narrow channel. But
moving from that almost unaccompanied solo to the full-bodied
symphony of *Henry IV*, Shakespeare celebrates the 'modern' Renaissance, the Elizabethan spirit at its most bounteous and exuberant. In
Henry IV the whole man, exemplified by gallants like Raleigh and
Sidney, lives his multiple life; in Hal that life is being lived, as in the
play's vast range all of Elizabethan England seems to be living.

Thus one feels called upon to say that nothing in *Henry IV* is inert
or unrealized. Rather, everything leaps to instant, teeming life. Like
this moment of England itself, Shakespeare's medium is assured
enough to encourage his characters and their actions to be genius-
like themselves. There is, consequently, something in the individual
personae and in their engagements of the rhythm of the dance,
movement altogether itself. But of course it is modern dance one
thinks of, not a court dance. The movement of earlier plays in their
stately, artificial symmetry contrasts sharply with the naturalness, the
crackling immediacy, of *Henry IV*'s development. In fact, so
crammed and bustling is the play in its use of a language adaptive to
all occasions—those of the court, the tavern, the street, the battlefield, lovers—each occasion seemingly wrapped up in its own skin
and breath, that not until quite recently have critics been able to see it
for the amazing whole it is. The richness, the brio, of *Henry IV* has
been ascribed to its nationalistic and patriotic, not to say epical, concerns. Certainly, the play most cogently testifies, this is a young
nation breaking loose, joyous in the mere rehearsal of its newly
released powers. The work's greatness resides in its very impurity, its
gallimaufry-like nature, its bursting of normal bounds.

And critics have gradually become apprised of this freedom, but no
less of the extraordinary form responsible for this freedom. Thus so
much in modern criticism has been made of the play's multiple structure, of the way in which scenes, one after another, collaborate and comment on each other, a balancing so daring that one scene seems to be,
not merely the counterpart of the other, but its subplot, that little more
need be said about it here. But the critical vehemence produced by the
tavern scenes and their master, Falstaff, must be dealt with. This vehemence has continued for some centuries. Ironically enough, however,
perhaps even more than with Shylock, it has been almost equally spent

on opposite positions: on the one hand, those who consider Falstaff not only the play's central figure but heroic and, for the abuse he sustains at the end of Part II, tragic as well; on the other, those who excoriate him as a ruffian, a vice, a Satan, to say the least a seducer of the young. But a creation of such magnitude and, simultaneously, of such intimately existential impact yields to no single view, no summary or generalizing. When we try to talk about him apart from his play we are bound to reduce him and so lose him. Whatever his moral worth, he rises, at least until Part II, fat singing dolphin that he is, above the element he lives in; and brimming it to flooding, he intoxicates us with that vintage sack. The intoxicating sack that his wit alone can make of it. Once a lord, he is now the chief lord of delight in a wakening in some sort the reverse of Sly's; he too enjoys a gallery of lusty pictures—impromptus and tableaux—but usually of his own devising. So, generation after generation, because of the sacred, earthy life in him, we, according to the bias of our own temperaments, passionately join or passionately disavow his company. Capable of every eventuality, he enables us to reflect another—maybe, if we are lucky and lively ourselves, even a new—iridescent side of his cornucopious nature. And therefore of our own. If he can animate creatures like Shallow and Slender it is not excessive to expect him to do the same for us.

Much like the contrary views of him is the extreme to which many modern critics have been led by their admiration for the Falstaff scenes. Considering him betrayed, they take his remarks and scenes to be, not only a puncturing of courtly hypocrisy parading as patriotism, but the play's essential meaning. For modern men with their belief mainly in the 'natural', carried to the point where only self-interest and submission to the appetites seem honest, such interpretation is pretty inevitable. Of course, the most faithful reading of the play attests that Falstaff and his scenes do have a fundamental, if low and therefore limited, seriousness that must be reckoned with; and of course, they expose the frivolity and the selfishness hidden away in the high scenes under thick brocades of words no less than of dress. The play's comics, like the zany, intricate carvings in cathedral doors and pews and like those cathedrals' gargoyles, do their part in exorcising evil and in draining off excess by expressing it. But necessary though this exposure may be, rather than fatally damaging those high scenes, it brings us to the reality inside them and, by throwing it into low relief, it helps us to realize it.

—Theodore Weiss, "Now of All Humours: *Henry IV, Parts I and II*," in *The Breath of Clowns and Kings: Shakespeare's Early Comedies and Histories* (New York: Atheneum, 1971), pp. 260–297. Reprinted in *Shakespearean Criticism* 30. Marie Lazzari, ed. (Detroit: Gale, 1991): pp. 73–74.

[In this excerpt, Black explores the way in which "figure turns
to form"; in other words, the evolution of the vision apparent
in the text into that which is depicted on the stage.]

If we put ourselves in the shoes of naive spectators viewing the play for
the first time without having read it, and seeing what Shakespeare has
contrived that we see, what does this spectacle of the bodies offer? We
have, as naive spectators, concentrated upon the primary and long-
awaited combat between the two young men. We have seen Hal's total
conviction that Falstaff is dead (and when has Falstaff ever before been
so totally silent? Short winded as he is, see [III.iii.159–60], he even in
sleep fetches his breath hard and snorts like a horse [II.iv.528–29]; it is a
remarkable feat for him to lie so quiet and so still). We have heard the
eulogies and still hear them as we look at the bodies—it is possible after
all, as Sonnet 23 says, "To hear with eyes." Now we see Hotspur and Falstaff lie together as if dead, both "in blood" (it is not the first time in the
play that Falstaff has contrived to wear some blood for effect). As we
watch and perhaps reflect,

>   Falstaff *riseth up.*

This is a superb stroke of visual artistry. The gasp of surprise among
first-time spectators of the play may still be heard in any theater where
it is staged as Shakespeare wrote it to be staged. No one brought freshly
through the experience of *Part One* up to this moment can know that
Falstaff has been alive all along (Falstaffs who wink or mug on the
ground as Hal speaks out his eulogy are not "[playing] out the play" as it
should be done).

In his rising, Falstaff overturns the securities which Hal's battle has
engendered. The audience had just been assured of "truth" and of the true
prince. But now Falstaff, who a moment before was "the true and perfect
image" of death, apologizes for his life and his deceit: "To counterfeit
dying, when a man thereby liveth, is to be no counterfeit, but the true and
perfect image of life indeed" [V.iv.17–19]. Along with the faint hint of
blasphemy on the theme of "losing" one's life to save it, there also is a
creepy logic to Falstaff's words; for if he is alive after his fall and his epi-
taph, may not Hotspur be alive as well? The nervous amusement in this
moment quickly is stilled when we see what Falstaff proceeds to do to Hotspur's body. "Therefore, sirrah, with a new wound in your thigh"
[V.iv.127–29], he says, suiting action to the words. The wound in the thigh
has a quality not merely of "hitting below the belt": it ensures an appropriate amount of blood from the artery in the inside upper leg—Hal spoke
of embowelling or embalming, and Falstaff has picked up the word; an
embalmer would draw blood from a major artery. But as well as yielding
blood to substantiate Falstaff's claim, attacking the corpse in this way
makes visual and gives ghastly substance to an especial horror of war

which supposedly was committed in Wales and reported from there. We may recall that in I. i. the King relayed an account of

> A thousand of [Mortimer's] people butchered,
> Upon whose dead corpse there was such misuse,
> Such beastly shameless transformation,
> By those Welsh women done, as may not be
> Without much shame retold or spoken of.
> [I.i.42–6]

"Such beastly shameless transformation . . . as may not be . . . retold" minces the matter. But what could not formerly be spoken of straightforwardly now is seen, as Falstaff the camp-follower so explicitly violates the corpse and robs it of the honor just conferred. There have been many robberies in the play, some of them actual and some figurative: Gad's Hill, the picking of Falstaff's pocket while *he* lay helpless, the "theft" of the kingdom ("And then I stole all courtesy from heaven . . . " [III.ii.50]) and of Hotspur's life ("O Harry, thou hast robb'd me of my youth!" [V.iv.77]). But all of these had at least some element of daring, or of fun. There is neither daring nor fun in the looting of Hotspur's last honors and dignity; what Hal has given, Falstaff disgracefully takes away.

Nor do the indignities perpetuated upon Hotspur end there. Falstaff now *Takes Hotspur on his back* and carries him, either off-stage to re-enter in a few moments, or about the rear of the stage as Hal and Prince John make their entrance. They speak a line or two, then see Falstaff come up to them. Their first reaction is amazement, not at Falstaff's burden which being behind him is mainly obscured by his bulk, but at his being alive (or a ghost). Hal's surprise is the audience's of a few minutes before:

> I saw [Falstaff] dead,
> Breathless and bleeding on the ground. Art thou alive?
> Or is it fantasy that plays upon our eyesight?
> I prithee speak, we will not trust our eyes
> Without our ears: thou art not what thou seem'st
> [V.iv.133–37]

Falstaff continues to treat the corpse with indignity, probably throwing it down. At the end of his lying account of how they "rose both at an instant, and fought a long hour by Shrewsbury clock" [V. iv. 147–48] (which echoes Hotspur's doubtless spurious tale of how Mortimer "did confound the best part of an hour / In changing hardiment with great Glendower" [I.iii.100–01]); Hal tells him to take up the body more fittingly—"Come, bring your luggage nobly on your back" [V.iv.156])—and the scene ends with Falstaff, alone, hefting up and carrying out the undoubtedly now much-battered corpse of Hotspur.

Hal has just called that corpse "luggage," the luggage of an army, which usually was hauled about by pack-train. As we see Falstaff first get the dead man on his back and march about with him, then toss him down, and at last resume the burden, we surely are meant to be reminded in a pitying way of Hotspur's great and informing vision of himself—alive, crested, and mounted in chivalric splendour:

> That roan shall be my throne
> Well, I will back him straight.
> [II.iii.70–1]

> And when I am a-horseback, I will swear. . . .
> [II.iii.101]

> Come let me taste my horse,
> Which is to bear me like a thunderbolt
> Against the bosom of the Prince of Wales.
> [IV.i.119–21]

Now all that chivalric vision has dwindled to this physical degradation. As I have said, Shakespeare's procedure in *Henry IV* is to set figure—the visions we hear about—against form—the actualities that we see. We actually see Hotspur "mounted" only upon the back of Falstaff, who has recruited the dead man into his last and most monstrous lie in *Part One* and who already has said,

> Hal, if I tell thee a lie, spit in my face,
> call me horse.
> [II.iv.193–94]

This is our last sight of Hotspur, and it is a terrible parody—a concrete parody—of the vision he has woven about himself, and a tragic final answer to the question asked of him earlier and answered so flippantly: "What is it carries you away?" [II.iii.75]. And all this while it was supposed to have been Hal who was "violently carried away [by] an old fat man" [II.iv.446–48].

Just as Hal gave honour to Hotspur, so also does he allow Falstaff to take—to steal—the honour of having killed Hotspur. After his initial amazement at Falstaff's reappearance, he seems to see through Falstaff's story. His use of the word "gild" in warranting that story indicates that he knows he is not guaranteeing true coin: "If a lie may do thee grace, I'll gild it with the happiest terms I have" [V.iv.157–58]. The Chief Justice's suspicions in *Part Two* lead him to use just the same word to Falstaff's face: "Your day's service at Shrewsbury hath a little gilded over your night's exploit on Gad's Hill" [I.ii.148–49]. Even Hal's generosity in allowing Falstaff's claim diminishes Hotspur, who at the least would have asked for a worthy and certain conqueror—Samuel Johnson [in *The Vanity of Human Wishes*] illustrates the vanity of human wishes with the military case of Charles XII, whose anticlimactic "fall was destined to . . . a dubious hand."

So Falstaff will strut through *Henry IV, Part Two* as the conqueror of Hotspur, as in fact a kind of spurious Hotspur (we may now recall that on Gad's Hill he bellowed Hotspur-like for *his* horse, *Part One* [II.ii.28–41]). In his posturing he will weave about himself his own kind of dream, one not necessarily of chivalry but certainly of power and wealth, of a state wherein "the laws of England are at [his] commandment" [*Henry IV, Part II*, V.iii.136–37]. As I have shown elsewhere [in "Counterfeits of Soldiership in *Henry IV*," *Shakespeare Quarterly*, 24 (1973), 372–82], Hal, the only man who knows for sure what really happened at Shrewsbury, overcomes this counterfeit Hotspur as conclusively as he overcame the real one. He does so in a scene which also is visually impressive. Falstaff, capering and sweating in his excitement, is dressed in his old and travel-stained clothes as he awaits the new King's entrance. His appearance is heavily stressed:

> *Falstaff.*
> O if I had had time to have made new liveries ... But 'tis no matter, this poor show doth better, this doth infer the zeal I had to see him . . . It shows my earnestness of affection— ... My devotion— ... As it were, to ride day and night, and not to deliberate, not to remember, not to have patience to shift me— ... But to stand stained with travel, and sweating with desire to see him, thinking of nothing else, putting all affairs else in oblivion, as if there were nothing else to be done but to see him.
> *Pistol.*
> 'Tis *semper idem* ...
>
> [*2 Henry IV*, V.v.10–28]

How very like Hotspur's is the impulsiveness that Falstaff would suggest—to ride day and night, not to deliberate, not to remember, not to have patience, thinking of nothing else, putting all affairs else into oblivion. But this is no fit counterpart to, or companion for, Henry V. Pistol's reassurance, "*Semper idem*" (ever the same), is ironic. Falstaff metaphorically, literally, visually, is unchanged. But the new King Henry's first words have been about the change which has come over him: "This new and gorgeous garment, majesty, Sits not so easy on me as you think" [V.ii.44–5]. And as the King now appears, wearing his coronation robes, the distance between what he has become and what this scruffy old man still is is pathetically visible; banishment is *seen* to be inevitable. Once he has been rejected, the only thing Falstaff has left in common with Hotspur is that his final exit is made in ignominious and painful silence: it is superfluous to note that he too is at the last "carried" away, to the Fleet [V.v.91].

—James Black, "*Henry IV*: A World of Figures Here," in *Shakespeare: The Theatrical Dimension*. Philip C. McGuire and David A. Samuelson, eds. (New York: AMS Press, Inc., 1974), pp. 165–183. Reprinted in *Shakespearean Criticism* 39. Dana Ramel Barnes, ed. (New York: Gale, 1998): pp. 154–156.

JONATHAN CREWE ON REFORMING PRINCE HAL IN *PART 2*

[Jonathan Crewe teaches Renaissance literature and critical theory at Dartmouth University. In addition to many articles, his published works include *Unredeemed Rhetoric; Thomas Nashe and the Scandal of Authorship; Hidden Designs: The Critical Profession and Renaissance Literature;* and *Trials of Authorship: Anterior Forms and Poetic Reconstruction from Wyatt to Shakespeare.* In this excerpt, Crewe remarks upon the importance of "the parricidal moment" in Henry's succession as the revelation of "male agency . . . as a politicized psychology or psychologized politics of sovereign succession."]

Whatever initial effect of unintelligibility may be produced by the reform-action(s) of the Henry plays does not arise from any shortage of models and contexts, historical and otherwise, for Prince Hal's reform. Well-recognized models, which are neither fully discrete nor fully successive, include those of a New Testament theology of the "new man," of medieval psychomachia, of disciplinary humanist pedagogy, and even of ego-psychology. Coercive vectors of reform include those of Renaissance subject-formation, of censorship and "courtly" refinement in the public theater, and—broadly speaking—of what Norbert Elias has called the civilizing process. The dominant model that has been applied to Hal's reform is also, however, one that renders it less rather than more intelligible: this is the model of the prodigal son. The prodigal-model is a tellingly *failed* one partly because it is not a narrative of primogeniture—of the scapegrace *eldest* son who is nevertheless to be the sovereign inheritor—but if anything a narrative somewhat subversive of that rigorously "unjust" principle. It is above all a model that acknowledges no parricidal impulse or dynamic in the process of reform and hence of "legitimate" or "authentic" succession. If anything, once again, that dynamic is forestalled, or displaced into sibling rivalry and reconciliation, in the prodigal son story. This refusal in any sense to license parricide is the condition on which patriarchal law and order properly so called can be maintained.

The action (or inaction) of reform in the Henry plays conspicuously does take account of the parricidal moment in the process of sovereign succession. So, implicitly, do the chronicles in presenting the young Henry as a usurper-manqué who raises his hand against the paternal lawgiver in the person of the Chief Justice. So does *The Famous Victories,* in which Hal's impatience for his father's death is an explicit motif, assimilated to his general wildness. This parricidal recognition is accompanied in *2 Henry IV* by an increased emphasis, rising to the pitch of apocalyptic hysteria in a late speech by Henry IV, on Hal's "wildness" as covert murderous savagery rather than mere youthful excess. In the eyes of Henry, the ailing, threatened father, the son's wildness constitutes an unreformed interior that must always be socially dissimulated.

Correspondingly, any innocuous revelling or even show of reform on the part of Prince Hal will be taken as dissimulation, the hidden content of which can be expected to emerge once he has succeeded to the throne. Thus Henry IV prophesies a wild apocalypse brought on by the unreformed, and perhaps unreformable, prince:

> Harry the fifth is crown'd! Up, vanity!
> Down, royal state! All you sage counsellors, hence!
> And to the English court assemble now
> From every region, apes of idleness!
> Now, neighbour confines, purge you of your scum!
> Have you a ruffian that will swear, drink, dance,
> Revel the night, rob, murder, and commit
> The oldest sins the newest kind of ways?
>
> . . . .
> ... the fifth Harry from curb'd licence plucks
> The muzzle of restraint, and the wild dog
> Shall flesh his tooth of every innocent.
>
> . . . .
> O, thou wilt be a wilderness again,
> Peopled with wolves, thy old inhabitants!
>   (4.5.119–37)

Despite its prophetic hysteria, Henry's vision isn't wholly inconsistent with the expanded *potentiality* given in *2 Henry IV* to resistant wildness and the "need" to reform. Nor is it inconsistent with the threatened tragic declension of wildness from relatively harmless masquing and revelling in *1 Henry IV* to savagery in *2 Henry IV*. In other words, it is not just the issue of parricidal succession, but of a corresponding predatory "wildness" resistant to any transformation—a wildness anterior and *interior* to civility, to the process of lawful inheritance, and to legitimized political rule—that *2 Henry IV* appears to take more seriously than does its predecessor. As this issue surfaces, the historical contingencies of Bolingbroke's "parricidal" usurpation and Hal's wildness may seem increasingly to belong to an order of necessity—in which case Henry IV's prophecy may also begin to sound like hysterical denial.

Insofar as succession is conceived to be wild in *2 Henry IV*, and to be so of necessity, its dynamic may seem to originate or inhere in the male character or specifically male *agency*, not as a natural fact but as the consequence of what I have already referred to as a politicized psychology or psychologized politics of sovereign succession. It is this agency that is "missing" in *1 Henry IV*, and from the reform that would, in effect, make Hal the inheritor in a theater-state. Under the "post-theatrical" regime of *2 Henry IV*, the sovereign inheritor will be required to reform in order to legitimize himself, but will also (contradictorily) be required not to reform in order to succeed. Moreover, the paternal demand for reform will seem like an effort to forestall rather than facilitate succession by taming—emasculating—the sovereign inheritor. Under these circumstances, Hal's constant anticipation and *deferral* of reform become intelligible, as do his curious paralysis and avoidance of his father. Yet it is not through Prince Hal and his father alone that the difficulties or even contradictions of reform are precipitated out in the play. Falstaff is exultantly unreformed and unreformable; he and his cronies, fond recallers of their wild youth, help at least as much as do Prince Hal and his father to unpack reform in the play.

At one level, the Falstaff-Shallow-Silence episodes function as a wickedly satirical exposure of "original" male deficiency rather than wild excess. There is no need to belabor the point that the wild youth of Shallow and Silence is a nostalgically recalled condition, denied by their contemporary, Falstaff. Their wild youth as unreformed students belongs to a commonplace nostalgic script, beloved of the law-abiding elderly. No need either to belabor the point that, insofar as Falstaff has claims to be the real wild man of the play, he is a wild *old* man. If anything, wildness is more plausibly the social condition of the old man than the young one, and it is more plausibly a function of social denial, marginalization, and conscious impotence than of any supposedly untamed or untamable excess in the "true" male character. In this satirically reductive setting, the name of Fall-staff speaks him no less than do those of Shallow and Silence.

The genuinely funny satirical comedy, as distinct from festive heartiness, of the Falstaff-Shallow-Silence episodes may thus seem to contest the "wild" male character and its ontological violence of agency as well as the process of succession in which it is justifyingly subsumed. Yet the zero-point of final reduction is one at which we never quite arrive. Or, more accurately, the satirical vanishing-point of "wild" maleness turns out to be indistinguishable from its mythic origin, glimpsed in and through Falstaff's alleged recall of the young Shallow:

> I do remember him at Clement's Inn, like a man made after supper of a cheese-paring. When a was naked, he was for all the world like a forked radish, with a head fantastically carved upon it with a knife. A was so forlorn, that his dimensions to any thick sight were invisible; a was the very genius of famine, yet lecherous as a monkey, and the whores called him mandrake.

> (3.2.302–09)

What this strange "recall" produces is a subhuman or inhuman grotesque of indeterminable sex, or of no sex at all, like the bare, forked animal Lear thinks he sees on the heath. (The apparition here is fully in keeping with Elizabethan folklore regarding the mandrake root: it can look male, female, or androgynous; human or non-human.) Apparently open to any construction—or to no determinate one—the root-like apparition of the young Shallow may all too literally mock any aspiration to get to the root of the matter of reform in terms of gendered character. What we find at the end of the line is literally a root.

At the critical moment, however, the interposition of a "thick-sighted" observer relativizes and equivocates any ontological determination. Furthermore, while the stark-naked Shallow is seen from the start as a remainder—a cheese-paring—rather than a bodily totality, and while he is always and already subsumed in an order of figurative likeness—he is cheese-like, radish-like—this characterization through deficiency is tantamount to masculine *recharacterization* in terms of insatiable appetite rather than substance or "matter." Appropriately, it is Falstaff who effects this particular recharacterization. He assimilates any male sexual deficiency to a psychic and bodily economy of "prior" starvation, while, as characteristically, he recalls Shallow in the guise of an edible vegetable—a garden radish—and thus as an object as well as subject of insatiable appetite. It is left to the whores to translate this garden radish (ironically?) into the exotic and erotically mythologized mandrake root. Exotic sexual desire is thus superinduced upon domestic appetite in a novel etiology of the ontologically violent male character. It is evidently in terms of this prior "deprivation" and consequent appetite that greedy Falstaff not only resists reform, but considers himself entitled (and driven) by "law of nature" (3.2.326) to make a regal mouthful of such dace as Shallow—or Prince Hal as inheritor of the kingdom. If it were to be suggested that Falstaff fails in his more extravagant ambitions because he is captive to a dysfunctional conception of ontological necessity and empowerment, it should be recalled that an intuition of the same drive may inform Henry IV's prophecy that Hal's reign will be one of unbridled appetite: "fleshing the tooth on every innocent."

The point to be made here is that the "need" to reform as well as the sources of resistance to it remain curiously undetermined *and* overdetermined in *2 Henry IV* without ceasing to be invoked as crucial to the play's action(s) and outcome(s). I have already suggested that this situation gains a certain intelligibility if it is critically linked to what I have called a psychologized politics or politicized psychology of masculine sovereignty; this linking does not constitute an explanation so much as an attempt to (re)situate the problem where it belongs. At a minimum, the "return" of an ontological violence seemingly displaced from *1 Henry IV* is at issue in *2 Henry IV*, as it is in *Julius Caesar* and *Hamlet*. That this attempt to resituate isn't wholly misplaced is suggested by the terms in which Hal's "reform" and the royal succession are finally staged—or perhaps, *faute de mieux*, stage-managed.

—Jonathan Crewe, "Reforming Prince Hal: The Sovereign Inheritor in *2 Henry IV*," in *Renaissance Drama, New Series XXI: Disorder and the Drama.* Mary Beth Rose, ed. (Evanston, IL: Northwestern Univ. Press, 1990), pp. 230–234.

[In this excerpt, Bennett suggests that cyclical views of history
in *Part 2* and in Chehkov's *The Cherry Orchard* occupy a
moment of transition between cultural eras. In Shakespeare's
play, the moment is "a precious pause of fellowship and natural
harmony" amidst "war, fatigue, disease, death, and rejection."]

Within the four-play cycle of the Henriad, *The Second Part of Henry the
Fourth* depicts a world of secular time that has been exhausted by war.
The powers of leadership have been depleted by sickness and death,
leaving the outcome of human events increasingly to forces of nature:
time and chance. Divorced from the stabilizing and nurturing roots of
natural succession by Henry's usurpation of Richard, the political state
along with its tenuously situated monarch has been sapped of its
strength through the hectic disease of civil war and is, in effect, mori-
bund. Shakespeare reminds us, though, that not all the little pockets of
society, peopled by ordinary folk, are uprooted from their traditional
ways and daily lives by the strife of persons in power. Although several
times in the course of these plays troops have marched through
Gloucestershire and soldiers have been recruited, the justices, "good
cousin Shallow" and "good cousin Silence," when not interrupted by
these rare and brief intrusions, find goings-on of family—wife,
daughter, nephew—and the price of schooling at Oxford more relevant
conversation. This is not to say that their world on a daily basis is a
golden world, nor that they are unfallen inhabitants. Shakespeare has
no intention of veering unrealistically into a pastoral idyll. The idealized rustic, Corin, belongs in the fictional Arden of *As You Like It* while
the dull and complacent Shallow and Silence belong to the actual
Gloucestershire. In the two plays written at the same time, Shakespeare
distinguishes between romantic pastoral and historical pastoral.
Shallow and Silence, like Pistol and the other comic low life of this play,
are humors characters, whose names reflect their personalities. They
are guilty of all the human inadequacies that Dover Wilson and Derek
Traversi find in forming Shakespeare's conception of them, and yet
Robert Ornstein is also right in observing how they can comfortably
"speak of the unchanging certainties of rural life" in contrast to the
exhausting vicissitudes of the high and mighty. It is a matter of choice
whether one wants to emphasize the deficiencies of morals, mind, and
spirit of these country functionaries ("Justice, in fact, as Shallow exer-
cises it, is close, narrow, and mean in the defence of petty interests"); or
the halcyon quality of their country life ("an air of homey comfort, the
air of provincial old England"). Shakespeare's characteristically balanced design denies priority to either the sentimental or the cynical
response, and this tempered, benign vision is a quality to which more
than any other Chehkov is Shakespeare's heir. Yet as the drama progresses through the three Gloucestershire scenes, one senses the growing

influence of nature as the political world, to which the rural world is foil, crumbles.

The scenes between Shallow and Falstaff chart nature's reclaiming ever so briefly the humanity of Falstaff from his imprisoning self-fashioned identity of a man with a bright future, being, as he would have us and himself believe, the vigorous and influential compatriot of Prince Hal. The "youthful" Sir John first enters Gloucestershire to do some lucrative recruiting on his way to the battle front (III.ii.). In this encounter with the justices, to which Silence contributes only ten words, Falstaff seems to be hardly of their company, superior to them both in wit and energy. We expect no less distance in energy and attitude between Falstaff and the justices when Falstaff determines after Gaultree Forest to return to London via Gloucestershire with a mind toward gulling Shallow of some much needed cash. Surprisingly, though, Falstaff seems a mere accessory in his second appearance (V.i.). Whereas earlier Falstaff, the recruiting officer, presided over the action, here he stands quietly by as Shallow and Davy carry out the routine business of the shire from planting to petty bribery. Falstaff barely says a word until his closing soliloquy in which he assesses the world he has observed, and underneath his complacent mockery we discern a feature of this world that is common to the golden world, namely, the leveling of social differences. "It is a wonderful thing," Falstaff observes after watching Justice Shallow and his man, Davy, interact,

> to see the semblable coherence of his men's spirits and his. They, by observing him, do bear themselves like foolish justices; he, by conversing with them, is turn'd into a justice-like servingman. Their spirits so married in conjunction with the participation of society that they flock together in consent, like so many wild geese. (V.i.64–71)

The class system exists, but life in the country is so basic that the gap between master and servant is negligible, so it seems.

While the first two Gloucestershire scenes distinguish the country from the court without romanticizing the former, they hardly prepare us for the charming golden moment of the orchard scene. As the third scene of Act Five opens, we see the orchard through Falstaff's eyes and look with surprise at the natural pleasures of the place. It disarms our smug sense of superiority over these foolish rural justices and their company. The orchard setting where they will eat its fruit, "last year's pippin of [Shallow's] own graffing," is conventionally Edenic. It is dusk presumably as three old men relax after supper, and the play's dominant motif of death takes on an Arcadian tinge. In the persons of the aged revellers mortality broods gently over the scene. Song, albeit in the form of trite ditties, provides in Shakespeare's whimsical fashion, a lyrical quality to the scene. The old king is dead, although the revellers do not know it, and the new king is not yet crowned. Time has stopped for a while; chronicle history yields to lyrical interlude. Falstaff's first

substantive words to Hal in the previous play, "When thou art king . . . ,"
revealed him to be ever alert to his own political interests when in Hal's
company, but here he seems for the moment cleansed of patronizing
contempt and political calculation as one struck honest by a sudden
revelation: "'Fore God, you have here goodly dwelling and rich" (V.iii.6).
These first words on his entering the orchard ring true and candid, the
response to a world of basic pleasures of nature hitherto unknown to
him. No cunning or ulterior motive need be sought behind his
response to the merry songs of Silence, "There's a merry heart! Good
Master Silence, I'll give you a health for that anon" (23–24). For the first
time since we have known him, Falstaff has abandoned, or been shorn
of, pretenses and can enjoy the company of persons his own age. The
scene is that of an old men's saturnalia, convivial, precious, genuinely
gay but brief like the time remaining for these men. This holiday world,
unlike that of the Boar's Head Tavern, is rooted in nature, not wit. As
Hal's appearance in the tavern was its occasion for holiday, so Falstaff's
presence in Gloucestershire is the occasion for the justices' celebration;
but whereas the young Hal takes the tavern by storm, releasing an ocean
of pent up frustrations, Falstaff's role in the orchard is uncommonly
sanguine and subdued. Before the entry of Pistol, which ends the interlude, Shallow speaks twenty-five lines, Silence, the newly crowned lord
of misrule, speaks and sings twenty-two, and Falstaff's modest
responses take up only nine. In the inversion of norms that sets the saturnalian golden world apart from the world of time, in Justice Shallow's
orchard, on this occasion, Vanity is silenced and Silence sings.

As in the tavern so in the orchard, holiday ends with the intrusion of
a messenger with news from the court. The mood and occasion of the
supper is spoiled by the arrival of Pistol. Ironically, Pistol's "good" news
of the king's death calls Falstaff back to his world of illusion, now that
Hal is king. In this heady moment of perceived power, Falstaff sullies
the meaning of friendship by reducing it merely to a means for
advancement as he anticipates unchecked authority under the new king.
Yet at the same time, the orchard experience just past seems to have left
its impression, as Justice Shallow, heretofore merely a fool to be duped,
seems elevated to chief among Falstaff's friends: "Master Robert
Shallow, choose what office thou wilt in the land, 'tis thine . . . be what
thou wilt, I am Fortune's steward! . . . Blessed are they that have been my
friends, and woe to my Lord Chief Justice!" (125–40). Hal's vow of allegiance to the Lord Chief Justice in the previous scene only serves to
make Falstaff's lawless expectations pathetic, not threatening, and the
cessation of the true golden moment by the introduction of an illusory
one is made explicit by the aureate terms in which Pistol proclaims his
supposed good news: "And tidings do I bring, and lucky joys, / And
golden times, and happy news of price . . . I speak of Africa and golden
joys" (95–100). Silence sings his last line of Robin Hood and his merry
men (cf. the wrestler Charles' association of Robin Hood with the
golden world in *AYL:* I.i.116–20), and then returns to the state of being
for which his name is signature, as the same wine which inspired his

lyrics now puts him to sleep. Word of the new king recommences history, leaving the scene of three old men in an orchard of an evening, a precious pause of fellowship and natural harmony in a play dominated by war, fatigue, disease, death, and rejection.

—Robert B. Bennett, "The Golden Age in the Cycles of History: Analogous Visions of Shakespeare and Chekov," *Comparative Literature Studies* 28, no. 2 (1991): pp. 165–169.

MATTHEW H. WIKANDER ON HAL'S "UNKNOWABLE REAL SELF"

[Matthew H. Wikander is Professor of English and Director of the Liberal Studies Program at the University of Toledo (Ohio). He is author of *Princes to Act: Royal Audience and Royal Performance, 1578–1792*. In this excerpt, Wikander discusses the way in which Hal achieves his objective, to become master of his situation and an icon of legitimate rule.]

"Go, you thing, go!" Falstaff dismisses the hostess in *Part 1*. "Say, what thing? what thing?" she cries, and when Sir John calls her a beast, she pursues the issue: "Say, what beast, thou knave, thou?" "What beast? Why an otter." "An otter, Sir John," Prince Hal interrupts, "why an otter?" "Why? she's neither fish nor flesh, a man knows not where to have her" (III.iii.115–16,124–28). Yet it is not the hostess but Hal who has been the amphibian in the play. Here in III.iii, he has just returned from convincing his father of his loyalty and zeal. He is flourishing in both of his environments, the tavern and the court.

The amphibian has its own complex range of suggestion. "[P]oor monster," Viola pronounces herself, neither man nor woman; her brother, lost at sea, was last glimpsed "like [Arion] on the dolphin's back," in amphibious linkage (*Twelfth Night* II.ii.34, I.ii.15). ⟨ . . . ⟩ Viola's sentiment here is in sympathy with the antitheatrical writings of the period, with their rejection of disguise and repudiation of the amphibious boy actors of the public stage. More vigorously aligned with that tradition of antitheatrical thinking is Jonson's representation of Morose's house of babble, a cacophonous theater in which the key revelation turns on the person of the boy actor himself. On the other hand, Hal, until he repudiates "the thing I was," seems content to be an otter; like Francis the apprentice shuttling from one room to another, he is continually promising "Anon, anon" while shuttling between his two worlds.

The linkage between the otter, the "thing" that Hal was, and the boy actor points towards an indeterminacy in Hal. Like the boy actor or the apprentice, he is at a liminal phase of his development, neither fish nor flesh. ⟨ . . . ⟩

⟨ . . . ⟩ Hal's repudiation of the "thing" he was, of his festive or amphibious other self, postulates an unknowable real self, a true self, that has been concealed throughout his two plays and that may, indeed, remain unknowable in Henry V. Hamlet, rejecting the "actions that a man might play" and insisting upon "that within which passes show," pushes antitheatricalism further (*Hamlet* I.ii.84–85). He refuses to be known theatrically—by his actions, his cloak, his sighs, his tears. "Theatre has mimesis, not as its method, but as its subject matter," David Cole has argued. Building on Barish and Cole, it is possible to argue that expressions of antitheatrical sentiments by characters in plays constitute a playwright's critique of theatrical mimesis. The unease we feel about the Protean Hal is an unease about theatrical mimesis, written into the plays. To the extent that Hal is a kind of otter, a cipher like Viola into whom significances can be all too easily read, criticism of Hal and of his reformation has tended to reveal rather the critics' attitudes toward mimesis than to pin down Hal's elusive essence.

While Prince Hamlet rejects utterly the proposition that a true self, an own self, can be publicly known, Prince Hal wants to be known most fully in his public self. "I do; I will," Hal announces in the Boar's Head tavern when Falstaff urges him that to "banish plump Jack" is to "banish all the world" (*1 Henry IV* II.iv.479–80). There is nothing of Hamlet's riddling uncertainty in the expression of this resolve. Hal has fully prepared the audience in the theater (as opposed to his drunken onstage audience) for his resolution in his famous first-act soliloquy:

> I know you all, and will a while uphold
> The unyok'd humor of your idleness.
> Yet herein will I imitate the sun,
> Who doth permit the base contagious clouds
> To smother up his beauty from the world,
> That when he please again to be himself,
> Being wanted, he may be more wond'red at,
> By breaking through the foul and ugly mists
> Of vapors that did seem to strangle him.
>   (I.ii.195–203)

Hamlet envisions self-revelation as impossible, but Prince Hal sees it as a cosmic *coup-de-théâtre* in which he will reveal himself to be at one with his iconic image, as the blessed sun of heaven, the son of England, the prodigal son returned—as, in short, the resolution of that impossible paradox, a Christian king. In his first soliloquy he proposes a narrative, a way of seeing his career, that transforms him into the answer to history's desire for fully legitimate authority.

—Matthew H. Wikander, "The Protean Prince Hal," in *Comparative Drama* 26, no. 4 (Winter 1992–93): pp. 297–301.

Plot Summary of
Henry V

Act I determines Henry's claim to France. In scene 1 the Bishop of Ely and the Archbishop of Canterbury discuss the piety and statecraft with which the newly ascended king has astounded both clergy and courtiers. About the young king's ribald past in the company of Falstaff, Ely observes, "The strawberry grows underneath the nettle, / And wholesome berries thrive and ripen best / Neighbor'd by fruit of baser quality; / And so the Prince obscur'd his contemplation / Under the veil of wildness, which (no doubt) / Grew like the summer grass, fastest by night, / Unseen, yet crescive in his faculty." The Archbishop suspects a miracle.

In scene 2 the Archbishop of Canterbury attempts to prove, in his "Sallic Law" speech, the legitimacy of Henry's claim to the throne of France. The Dauphin's ambassadors appear to offer an appeasement to Henry, who has already claimed in France "certain dukedoms, in the right / Of [his] great precedessor, King Edward the Third." The Dauphin's joke, a gift of tennis balls, becomes Henry's pretext to mount an invasion. His message to "the Dolphin" plays upon the joke: "When we have march'd our rackets to these balls, / We will in France, by God's grace, play a set / Shall strike his father's crown into the hazard. / . . . But I will rise there with so full a glory / That I will dazzle all the eyes of France. . . ."

In **Act II** Henry prepares to challenge his foe, the French king. He unmasks Scroop, Grey, and Cambridge as traitors in scene 2: "Hear your sentence. / You have conspired against our royal person, / Join'd with an enemy proclaim'd, and from his coffers / Received the golden earnest of our death; / . . . Get you therefore hence, / Poor miserable wretches, to your death." Henry immediately sets out for France, declaring "[T]he signs of war advance: / No king of England, if not king of France!"

Interspersed with the scenes of king and courtiers are brief scenes at the Boar's Head Tavern. In scene 3 Hostess Quickly describes to her husband, Pistol, the deathbed of Falstaff, at which, she says "I put my hand into the the bed and felt [his feet], and they were as cold as any stone; then I felt to his knees, and so upar'd and upar'd, and all was as cold as any stone." Pistol leaves for France to fight in service to Henry, bidding his wife to "Let huswifery appear: keep close, I thee command."

In scene 4 a messenger arrives at the court of the French King Charles VI with Henry's claim to the throne "derived / From his most famed of famous ancestors, / Edward the third" and bidding Charles "resign" his crown. Charles promises to provide his response the next day.

Act III opens with commentary by the Chorus asking us to suppose that the French ambassador "[t]ells Harry that the King doth offer him / Katherine his daughter, and with her, to dowry, / Some petty and unprofitable dukedoms." In scene 1 Harry urges Exeter, Bedford, and Gloucester "unto the breach . . . like so many Alexanders." And in scene 2 we see the less illustrious troops, Nym, Bardolph, and Pym joined by the drunken Macmorris and Captain Jamy. Scene 3 opens upon King Henry and his retinue before the walls of Harfleur. He waits to hear from the "governor" of the city on the matter of surrender. The governor admits that, because King Charles is not yet ready to fight, they will open their gates and submit to Henry's control. The action shifts to Katherine (scene 4) and Alice, "an old gentlwoman." Their dialogue, in French, is punctuated by the naming of body parts in comical, fractured English.

In scene 5 the King of France, upon learning that the English troops are "sick and famish'd in their march" from Harfleur, sends Mountjoy, the herald, to find "what willing ransom" King Henry "will give" to avoid the war that France intends to win. Montjoy arrives at the English encampment in Picardy (scene 6) to tell King Henry that his triumph at Harfleur was not the success it seemed: "Though we seem'd dead, we did but sleep," Montjoy warns him, since "advantage is a better soldier than rashness." Though Henry admits to the herald that his army is "but a weak and sickly guard," he will, if hindered, "your tawny ground with your red blood / Discolor. . . . / We would not seek a battle, as we are, / Nor, as we are, we say we will not shun it. / So tell your master."

The Chorus opens **Act IV**, the scene of his stunning victory at Agincourt, asking the audience to imagine the scene at the English encampment where, despite Henry's apparent confidence and the "cheerful semblance and sweet majesty" with which he encourages his men on this night before the battle at Agincourt, he knows that they are surrounded by a "dread" army. Unaware that he addresses King Henry, an English soldier confides his disillusionment with their cause (scene 1). He says that the king "hath a heavy reckoning to make, when all those legs, and arms, and heads, chopp'd off in a battle, shall join together at a latter day and cry all, 'We died at such a place.'" He suspects that, when all their "throats are cut, he [the king] may be ransom'd, and we ne'er the wiser." Henry admits that, if that is the case, he would "never trust his word after." Before the soldier leaves they exchange gloves as a challenge to continue their "quarrel" when they meet again. Henry promises that it will be "in the king's company."

At the French camp (scene 2) the Dolphin is confident of victory and, in scene 3, sends Montjoy to secure the English surrender. Henry's response to King Charles is that, though their "gayness" and "gilt are all besmirch'd / With rainy marching in the painful field," his soldiers' comfort and appearance will improve when they "pluck / The gay new coats o'er the French soldiers' heads." By scene 5, the French army is in ruins, and the Dolphin laments that "[r]eproach and everlasting shame / Sits mocking in our plumes."

In scene 7, Fluellen and Gower discuss how the French king had "caus'd every soldier to cut his prisoner's throat" before he and what was left of his troops had fled the battlefield. They recall that Alexander the Great had killed his best friend. Gower remarks, "Our King . . . never kill'd any of his friends." But Fluellen means only to compare

Alexander's act to Henry's more generous turning away of the reprobate Falstaff – without killing him. But Henry, angered by the murder of the English prisoners, orders the throats of their own prisoners to be cut. Montjoy comes to ask permission to remove the French dead from the field. Henry at last learns, from Montjoy, the name of the place of this battle, and declares, "Then call we this the field of Agincourt, / Fought on the day of Crispin Crispianus." Fluellen reminds him that, according to "the chronicles," Henry's great-uncle, the Prince of Wales, had also fought a "prave pattle" in France, and that Welshmen like Fluellen had fought with him. In this same scene Williams, with whom Henry had exchanged the glove, enters, looking for the soldier who had challenged him. King Henry sends first Williams, to seek out Gower, then Fluellen, with the glove tucked into his hat.

In scene 8 Williams recognizes the glove Fluellen wears and strikes him, believing it stolen from its perhaps murdered owner. King Henry enters upon the scene of their argument and claims the glove. Williams asks for pardon and Henry has the glove filled with crowns. An English herald enters with a paper that counts ten thousand French dead; another paper counts less than thirty English dead, including Edward, the duke of York. Although "not lawful" to do so, Henry will proclaim the body count "in procession to the village" as proof that "God fought for us."

Act V opens with the Chorus describing the joyous welcome for King Henry and his troops when they return to England. (The Chorus also apologizes for the author's license with historical fact.) Henry returned to France for a second campaign, and has just made a third invasion, the "back-return" that will lead to the treaty with which the play concludes, and to the union with Katherine.

Scene 2 is a meeting between King Henry, Exeter, Gloucester, Warwick, Westmerland, and other lords, and Queen Isabel, the king of France, the duke of Burgundy, Katherine, Alice, and other Frenchmen. Burgundy warns Henry that the French are exhausted in both spirit and resources. The "mangled Peace" has not brought an end to the "savagery" of the population or of the natural world. Henry responds that peace, "[w]hose want gives growth to the imperfections" Burgundy cites, can be achieved only "[w]ith full accord to all our just demands." Henry sends his brothers, Clarence and Gloucester, with Exeter, to discuss further the terms of the peace—but Katherine must stay. She is, Henry declares, "our capital demand, comprised / Within the fore-rank of our articles."

Alone with Katherine and Alice, Henry asks Kate, "Do you like me?" As she did in the earlier lesson in English, Alice helps to translate for Kate, and now also for Henry. Eventually, Kate agrees to marry him—if it will also please her father. It does, and the legitimacy of Henry V's rule is secured by the alliance. The king of France agrees to the marriage and observes that it will "raise up / Issue to me, that the contending kingdoms / Of France and England . . . / May cease their hatred; and this dear conjunction / Plant neighborhood and Christian-like accord / In their sweet bosoms, that never war advance / His bleeding sword 'twixt England and fair France." ❀

List of Characters in
Henry V

King Henry V is not a favorite with critics. He is here the ideal king but a surprisingly depthless hero. His royal sense of humor has dulled since *Henry IV,* as the exchange with Williams shows, but revives in his response to the Dauphin's gift of tennis balls, showing the self-assurance necessary to his position. He is at his best when performing patriotic functions and pursuing a just political cause. As he inspires his ill-equipped and exhausted troops at Harfleur and Agincourt, he is an ideal man of action and a great leader. His rhetoric does not seem the stuff of a subtle mind, but it reflects the patriotic fervor that is central to the play. His wooing of Katherine in the last act has been described as "ursine" and a blot upon the play.

Gower and **Fluellen** are, respectively, English and Welsh captains in King Henry's army. Their discussions provide background and context for many of the play's scenes. They are instrumental in constructing many humorous situations.

Katherine (Kate) is the daughter of the French King Charles and Queen Isabel. With her attending gentlewoman, Alice, she makes both a rhetorical and marital connection with England. When she finally agrees to marry Henry, we cannot be certain that she quite knows what she's done, but we know that the king will now have legitimate and secure power in France.

Humphrey, duke of Gloucester, John, duke of Bedford, and the **duke of Clarence** are brothers to the king.

Duke of Exeter is uncle to the king.

Duke of York is cousin to the king.

Charles the Sixth and **Queen Isabel** are king and queen of France. ❀

Critical Views on
Henry V

SAMUEL JOHNSON COMMENTS ON THE PLAY, 1765

[Samuel Johnson was one of the most eminent literary figures of the eighteenth century. An essayist, poet, translator, and reviewer, Johnson's works include *The Lives of the English Poets; The Vanity of Human Wishes;* and *Rasselas, Prince of Abyssinia.* We know him best through Boswell, his biographer, who wrote of his brilliant conversation, his eccentricities and opinionate polemics against many (including Scots, Whigs, and Americans), his interest in the supernatural, and his kindness, generosity, and largeness of spirit. In this excerpt, Johnson gives his usual shrewd and succinct response to a performance of the play.]

This play has many scenes of high dignity, and many of easy merriment. The character of the King is well supported, except in his courtship, where he has neither the vivacity of Hal, nor the grandeur of Henry. The humour of Pistol is very happily continued; his character has perhaps been the model of all the bullies that have yet appeared on the English stage.

The lines given to the chorus have many admirers; but the truth is, that in them a little may be praised, and much must be forgiven; nor can it be easily discovered why the intelligence given by the chorus is more necessary in this play than in many others where it is omitted. The great defect of this play is the emptiness and narrowness of the last act, which a very little diligence might have easily avoided.

—Samuel Johnson, *Notes on Shakespeare's Plays,* 1765.

AUGUST WILHELM SCHLEGEL ON THE CHORUS AS DRAMATIC DEVICE IN THE PLAY

[August Wilhelm Schlegel was a critic who lived from 1767–1845.]

King Henry the Fifth is manifestly Shakespeare's favourite hero in English history: he paints him as endowed with every chivalrous and kingly virtue; open, sincere, affable, yet, as a sort of reminiscence of his youth, still disposed to innocent raillery, in the intervals between his perilous but glorious achievements. However, to represent on the stage his whole history subsequent to his accession to the throne, was attended with great difficulty. The conquests in France were the only distinguished event of his reign; and war is an epic rather than a dramatic object. For wherever men act in masses against each other, the appearance of chance can never wholly be avoided; whereas it is the business of the drama to exhibit to us those determinations which, with a certain necessity, issue from the reciprocal relations of different individuals, their characters and passions. In several of the Greek tragedies, it is true, combats and battles are exhibited, that is, the preparations for them and their results; and in historical plays war, as the *ultima ratio regum*, cannot altogether be excluded. Still, if we would have dramatic interest, war must only be the means by which something else is accomplished, and not the last aim and substance of the whole. For instance, in *Macbeth*, the battles which are announced at the very beginning merely serve to heighten the glory of Macbeth and to fire his ambition; and the combats which take place towards the conclusion, before the eyes of the spectator, bring on the destruction of the tyrant. It is the very same in the Roman pieces, in the most of those taken from English history, and, in short, wherever Shakespeare has introduced war in a dramatic combination. With great insight into the essence of his art, he never paints the fortune of war as a blind deity who sometimes favours one and sometimes another; without going into the details of the art of war, (though sometimes he even ventures on this), he allows us to anticipate the result from the qualities of the general, and their influence on the minds of the soldiers; sometimes, without claiming our belief for miracles, he yet exhibits the issue in the light of a higher volition: the consciousness of a just cause and reliance on the protection of Heaven give courage to the one party, while the presage of a curse hanging over their undertaking weighs down the other. In *Henry the Fifth* no opportunity was afforded Shakespeare of adopting the last mentioned course, namely, rendering the issue of the war dramatic; but he has skillfully availed himself of the first.—Before the battle of Agincourt he paints in the most lively colours the light-minded impatience of the French leaders for the moment of battle, which to them seemed infallibly the moment of victory; on the other hand, he paints the uneasiness of the English King and his army in their desperate situation, coupled with their firm determination, if they must fall, at least to fall with honour. He applies this as a general contrast between the French and English national characters; a contrast which betrays a partiality for his own nation, certainly excusable in a poet, especially when he is backed with such a glorious document as that of the memorable battle in question. He has surrounded the general events of the war with a fulness of individual, characteristic, and even sometimes comic features. A heavy Scotchman, a hot Irishman, a well-meaning, honourable, but pedantic Welchman, all speaking in their peculiar dialects, are intended to show us that the warlike genius of Henry did not merely carry the English with him, but also the other natives of the two islands, who were either not yet fully united or in no degree subject to him. Several good-for-nothing associates of Falstaff among the dregs of the army either afford an opportunity for proving Henry's strictness of discipline, or are sent home in disgrace. But all this variety still seemed to the poet insufficient to animate a play of which the subject was a conquest, and nothing but a conquest. He has, therefore, tacked a prologue (in the technical language of that day *a chorus*) to the beginning of each act. These prologues, which unite epic pomp and solemnity with lyrical sublimity, and among which the description of the two camps before the battle of Agincourt forms a most admirable night-piece, are intended to keep the spectator constantly in mind, that the peculiar grandeur of the action described cannot be developed on a narrow stage, and they must, therefore, supply, from their own imaginations, the deficiencies of the representation. As the matter was not properly dramatic, Shakespeare chose to wander in the form also beyond the bounds of the species, and to sing, as a poetical herald what he could not represent to the eye, rather than to cripple the progress of the action by putting long descriptions in the mouths of the dramatic personages. The confession of the poet that "four or five most vile and ragged foils, right ill disposed can only disgrace the name of Agincourt," (a scruple which he has overlooked in the occasion of many other great battles, and among others of that of Philippi,) brings us here naturally to the question how far, generally speaking, it may be suitable and advisable to represent wars and battles on stage. The Greeks have uniformly renounced them: as in the whole of their theatrical system they proceeded on ideas of grandeur and dignity a feeble and petty imitation of the unattainable would have appeared insupportable in their eyes. With them, consequently, all fighting was merely recounted. The principle of the romantic dramatists was altogether different: their wonderful pictures were infinitely larger than their theatrical means of visible execution; they were every where obliged to count on the willing imagination of the spectators, and consequently they also relied on them in this point. It is certainly laughable enough that a handful of awkward warriors in mock armour, by means of two or three swords, with which we clearly see they take especial care not to do the slightest injury to one another, should decide the fate of mighty kingdoms. But the opposite extreme is still much worse. If we in reality succeed in exhibiting the tumult of a great battle, the storming of a fort, and the like, in a manner any way calculated to deceive the eye, the power of these sensible impressions is so great that they render the spectator incapable of bestowing that attention which a poetical work of art demands; and thus the essential is sacrificed to the accessory. We have learned from experience, that whenever cavalry combats are introduced the men soon become secondary personages beside the four-footed players. Fortunately, in Shakespeare's time, the art of converting the yielding boards of the theatre into a riding course had not yet been invented. He tells the spectators in the first prologue in *Henry the Fifth:* —

> Think, when we talk of horses, that you see them
> Printing their proud hoofs in the receiving earth.

When Richard the Third utters the famous exclamation, —

it is no doubt inconsistent to see him both before and afterwards constantly fighting on foot. It is however better, perhaps, that the poet and player should by overpowering impressions dispose us to forget this, than by literal exactness to expose themselves to external interruptions. With all the disadvantages which I have mentioned, Shakespeare and several Spanish poets have contrived to derive such great beauties from the immediate representation of war, that I cannot bring myself to wish they had abstained from it. A theatrical manager of the present day will have a middle course to follow: his art must, in an especial manner, be directed to make what he shows us appear only as separate groups of an immense picture, which cannot be taken in at once by the eye; he must convince the spectators that the main action takes place behind the stage; and for this purpose he has easy means at his command in the nearer or more remote sound of warlike music and the din of arms.

However much Shakespeare celebrates the French conquest of Henry, still he has not omitted to hint, after his way, the secret springs of this undertaking. Henry was in want of foreign war to secure himself on the throne; the clergy also wished to keep him employed abroad, and made an offer of rich contributions to prevent the passing of a law which would have deprived them of the half of their revenues. His learned bishops consequently are as ready to prove to him his indisputable right to the crown of France, as he is to allow his conscience to be tranquillized by them. They prove that the Salic law is not, and never was, applicable to France; and the matter is treated in a more succinct and convincing manner than such subjects usually are in manifestoes. After his renowned battles, Henry wished to secure his conquests by marriage with a French princess; all that has reference to this is intended for irony in the play. The fruit of this union, from which two nations promised to themselves such happiness in future, was the weak and feeble Henry VI., under whom every thing was so miserably lost. It must not, therefore, be imagined that it was without the knowledge and will of the poet that a heroic drama turns out a comedy in his hands, and ends in the manner of Comedy with a marriage of convenience.

—August Wilhelm Schlegel, *Lectures on Dramatic Art and Literature,* John Black, trans., 1809.

LARRY S. CHAMPION ON THE STRUCTURAL DEVICES OF THE PLAY

[In this excerpt, Champion asserts that *Henry V* is in many ways the most structurally complex of Shakespeare's histories, noting that he uses multiple plots, diverse settings, the chorus, and fixed characterizations to establish and maintain the broad perspective vital to the historical theme.]

Demonstrably in *1, 2 Henry IV* a combination of structural devices establishes a perspective of adequately broad scope for the historical theme which yet features a sufficiently detailed quality of characterization to provoke and sustain at least limited emotional involvement. Similar devices are utilized in *Henry V.* Shakespeare develops a stylized and highly patriotic theme throughout the three movements of the plot: the preparation for war, the combat itself, and the concluding of the peace. With the multiple plots, the diverse settings, the use of the chorus as a persistent pointing device, and the essentially fixed characterization, he establishes and maintains a broad perspective by blocking a close emotional rapport between the spectators and any individual character. At the same time, he labors carefully to make Henry a dramatically compelling figure. This quality he accomplishes through a brief but significantly placed soliloquy, through a constant focus upon Henry resulting from the diverse manners in which the surrounding characters view him, and through the consistent interweaving of thematically related episodes which suspend the spectators between the level of allegorical abstraction on the one hand and of absorption in character analysis on the other.

Breadth of perspective is once more achieved through the interweaving of several significant plot strands, in this instance drawn both from opposing nations and from different sociopolitical English strata. The struggle between England and France is depicted alternately from the view of English theologians, English aristocracy, King Henry, citizens of Eastcheap, English common soldiers, French aristocracy, and Princess Katherine of France. Five separate plot lines are involved. Henry V's pursuit of the war—both the preparation in England and the execution on the French battlefields—comprises approximately 40 percent of the total lines (1,264 of 3,146); the action of his French counterpart and the scene of their capitulation account for 21 percent (656); the dialogue of Nell Quickly and her cohorts makes up 6 percent (193); the scenes with Katherine, 8 percent (256). The fifth plot strand, 26 percent of the total lines (819), is a virtual microcosm of the nation—the English Gower, Welsh Fluellen, Irish MacMorris, and Scots Jamy; in these figures Shakespeare conspicuously reflects the diverse national components (the busied giddy minds) united against the common foe. Enhancing the broad angle of vision resulting from these multiple plot strands, no fewer than forty-two characters have speaking parts, a total in Shakespeare's canon second only to that of *2 Henry IV.* And the location of the action shifts abruptly from England to France. The act division established in the Folio (no scenes are marked) involves an English setting in act I—Henry's palace, the London streets, and Southampton—and a French setting for the remainder of the play— King Charles' palace, Harfleur, Rouen, Picardy, and Agincourt. The eight settings (actually a greater number if one considers the multiple locations within the two palaces and the opposing camps at Agincourt) create an almost kaleidoscopic effect, even for the eclectic Elizabethan stage.

The chorus, another feature not utilized extensively in Shakespeare's previous histories, establishes a tone of unmitigated patriotism, which in turn enhances the stylization of the play. The stage will be a kingdom, the actors princes and monarchs. "Warlike Harry [will] / Assume the port of Mars" (prologue, 5–6); he is the "mirror of all Christian kings" (II,6) who will lead the honor-seeking and expectant "youth of England" (I) against the trembling French who seek to avoid war through "pale policy" (14): "O England! model to thy inward greatness, / Like little body with a mighty heart" (16–17). We are told in act 3 of England's brave and majestical fleet (5, 16) filled with "cull'd and choice-drawn cavaliers" (24) who travel toward Harfleur and destiny. And in act 4 the chorus describes the "hum" of the two camps the evening before battle, the "confident and overlusty French" (18) and the "poor condemned English" (22) cheered by "a little touch of Harry in the night" (47):

> And so our scene must to the battle fly;
> Where—O for pity!—We shall much disgrace,
> With four or five most vile and ragged foils
> (Right ill disposed, in brawl ridiculous)
> The name of Agincourt.
>
> (48–52)

In the final act King Henry, "free from vainness and self-glorious pride" (20), returns to London and is welcomed by his subjects as a conquering hero, after which he returns to France to conclude negotiations for a treaty with the French king. The epilogue strikes the patriotic chord once more, referring to Agincourt as an event in which "most greatly lived / This star of England" (5–6). Indeed the lone qualifying moment to the consistently hyperbolic and monolithic tone established by the choric figure is the closing reference to the infant Henry VI and to those around him lusting for power who will subsequently lose France and make England bleed (12).

Still another structural feature designed to maintain the broad historical scene, through attention to multiple character interaction rather than individual character analysis, is the virtual absence of soliloquies and asides. While, with the exception of Richard III, no single individual in Shakespeare's previous history plays engages in such private moments to a major extent, the soliloquy does function significantly in those earlier stage worlds. Among the three Henry VI plays and the two Henry IV plays, for example, soliloquies and asides comprise more than 5 percent of the total lines in every instance; the percentage is over 6.5 percent in three and as high as 8.5 percent in one. In signal contrast *Henry V* features no asides and only six soliloquies for 2.5 percent. Only three of twenty-three scenes (as marked in modern editions) are involved, and Henry's soliloquies occur in a single scene preceding Agincourt. While that scene is critically important, the fact is that Henry is essentially an external characterization. The spectators are not for the most part permitted to share either his private responses or those of the surrounding figures to the decisions (moral and otherwise) which dictate the actions of the play; and considering the relatively extensive use of soliloquies in the preceding stage worlds, one must logically infer that the move is a deliberate one on Shakespeare's part.

The spectators, more specifically, are not permitted a glimpse of Henry's private reaction to the irony of the Church's offer, toward the wars in France, of "a greater sum / Than ever at one time the clergy yet / Did to his predecessors part withal" (I, i, 79–81) at the same time a bill is under consideration which would strip the Church of "the better half of our possession" (8). Henry could hardly be blind to the ploy, and the perceptive spectators must inevitably wonder whose giddy mind is being busied with foreign quarrels. In any case the resulting ambiguity is complex; Henry is either almost incredibly naive, or he is caught up in the emotional frenzy of national patriotism, or he is the master calculator able to conceal his own devious thirst for expansion and martial glory in the seeming tolerance of the vested interests of those around him. Similarly, the spectators do not share Henry's private thoughts concerning the Dauphin's presentation of tennis balls, a gift which brings to mind Hal's wilder days. Likewise they see only the furious courage of the King at Harfleur and only his official proclamation of victory following the battle at Agincourt. When Henry in Picardy hears the report that "one Bardolph, if your majesty know the man" (III, vi, 101–2), is likely to be executed for plundering a church, he is permitted not the least semblance of recognition of their former friendly acquaintance in the peremptory retort: "We would have all such offenders so cut off" (107–8). Least of all does the audience comprehend Henry's true feelings for Katherine of France. The offer of the princess is rejected prior to the siege of Harfleur (chorus, III,30–32), yet in act 5 he argues that he loves her cruelly (ii,202–3). As in act I there is never a private word to guide us between the two extremes of the spectrum. While Henry, then, delivers fully 31 percent of the lines in the play (1,054), over 750 more than those of the next highest figure (Fluellen, 298), he speaks virtually without soliloquy. With the exception of an eleven-line passage by the boy who guards the luggage at the English camp (IV, iv, 67–77) and a ten-line passage by Pistol (V, i, 80–89), no other character in the play addresses the spectators privately. Neither of these moments, moreover, is of psychological significance: in the one the boy merely pronounces Pistol a greater coward than Bardolph and Nym, both of whom have been hanged for pillaging, and in the other Pistol admits that "Honor is cudgell'd" from his limbs and that upon his return to England he will turn bawd and cutpurse.

Henry V utilizes the soliloquy and the aside to a smaller degree than any other work in Shakespeare's canon; in many respects a remarkably public play, it focuses upon the numerous interactions and confrontations of characters rather than the subtle complexities of an individual figure. With Henry appearing in such a predominant number of scenes the structure is somewhat akin to that of *Richard III* without the soliloquies. Rather than a persistent juxtaposition of the King's private and public face, the spectators observe only the King's public actions in a stage world crowded with virtual supernumeraries—thirty-three characters who appear in three scenes or fewer (nineteen in a single scene). Certainly not surprisingly the characterization is static. Henry may face progressively more difficult decisions in the kingship, but he does not develop in the course of the play; whatever his unrevealed motivations he is from first to last the firm but just English monarch for whom the good of the nation is inseparable from his personal fortunes. The Henry who seeks a satisfactory public rationalization for moving against the French in act I is the same Henry who carefully negotiates the political-romantic arrangement with Katherine in act 5. The retributively destructive anger which flashes at the arrival of the Dauphin's gift of tennis balls recurs when the French attack the English camp and murder the young boys who guard it. And the same mercy exercised for the common English soldier at Southampton is visited upon the French at Harfleur, just as the military discipline which leads him unhesitatingly to order the execution of the English traitors at Southampton is evidenced again in his firm leadership at Agincourt. The chronology of the events in the play obviously is vital to the historical narrative, but so monolithic is Henry's character that the sequence of his appearances is of no significance whatever. The most important of the secondary figures, though functioning at times to undercut the dominant pattern of Henry's heroic posture, are themselves no less uniform in quality: for example, the arrogant and somewhat dimwitted Dauphin, who at the very least is furiously nationalistic; the rather pallid and acquiescent Katherine, whose primary dramatic value is her difficulty in pronouncing the King's English; the English traitors who, properly chastened, praise the justice of their fate; the four Englishmen who reflect the various nationalities yoked in the struggle with a common enemy; the incorrigible Pistol whose expediential courage keeps him from the French sword if not from Fluellen's leek and whose return to England bodes no promise of a fortune clear of the law.

—Larry S. Champion, "The Maturity Perspective: King John, 1, 2 Henry IV, Henry V," in Perspective in Shakespeare's English Histories (Athens, GA: Univ. of Georgia Press, 1980), pp. 92–165

ANDREW GURR ON THE THEME OF BROTHERHOOD IN THE PLAY

[In the following excerpt, Gurr analyzes the theme of brotherhood as developed through the structure and language of *Henry V.*]

When Alexander Court enters in 4.1.81 and addresses his companion as 'brother John Bates' he gives emphasis to a feature of this play which is unique in all Shakespeare. Court is one of the three English soldiers who are given curiously ordinary and yet full names. There is no Wart or Mouldy in 4.1, nor any anonymous 'soldiers' or mere surnames in their entry direction. And they have the longest talk with Henry in the play. These three brother-soldiers, whose names signify that they are brothers in misfortune rather than true brothers, highlight a special concept in the play. Henry has talked with one group of three of his subjects already. Addressing the three conspirators in 2.2 had involved Henry in some acting, but it was a mask he soon threw off as he threw off theirs. His dismissal of his bedfellow Scroop to death in Act 2 matches the death of Falstaff in the same act as the closing of the last door on his solitary self. His talk with the three plain soldiers in 4.1 reverses the earlier scene. Where with the conspirators he had acted himself as he threw off their disguises, in this scene with the honest men Henry's mask stays on. He is not one of this band of brothers.

The term Alexander Court uses to John Bates has already recurred through the play. Court's term is a pointer to and a preparation for Henry's most celebrated claim in his Crispin's Day speech, to be brother with all his army. Henry's assertion of brotherhood at that point makes Agincourt unique in the play. It marks what was probably designed to be the most potent single factor in the English victory. His trenchant proclamation, that everyone who 'sheds his blood with me / Shall be my brother; be he ne'er so vile / This day shall gentle his condition' (4.3.61–3), is carefully set up by a host of other claims to brotherhood and kinship in the play, before and after the battle. Pistol might have had reason to regret that Le Fer did not scratch him first before surrendering. ⟨ . . . ⟩

⟨ . . . ⟩ It is true that the uniqueness of Henry's claim to brotherhood in the Crispin's Day speech is emphasised by its difference from his equivalent speech in the previous battle, at Harfleur, and by the weaknesses in the English army that are put on show at Harfleur. There the soldiers, retreating from the breach they have made, are heartened by the king's urging them to return to the breach, although their renewed attack has no better effect than the previous one. Harfleur does not fall to any attack by the English. It only falls when the Governor, after listening to Henry's threats, admits that his hope of relief by the Dauphin's forces has failed. And that victory ends with Henry admitting that his forces are weak and that he must retreat to Calais. It is hardly a promising precursor for Agincourt.

Brotherhood, however, grows in importance before that battle. The Eastcheap clowns have already sworn their own pact of brotherhood and fellowship after their quarrel in 2.1. Bardolph tries to make Pistol and Nym friends with the logical plea 'We must to France together; why the devil should we keep knives to cut one another's throats?' (73–4). Like horseleeches (2.3.43–4), they must thrive on French blood, not each other's. But in 3.7.44–7 Llewellyn refuses Pistol's request to intercede for the condemned Bardolph in terms which call this easy concept of brotherhood into question. Llewellyn takes up a rank-conscious posture, upholding virtue and saying 'For if, look you, he were my brother I would desire the duke to use his good pleasure and put him to execution.' The duke, followed by Henry himself when he hears of Bardolph's punishment, does not yet have any feeling of blood-brotherhood with the vile. That must wait for the battle speech itself.

The chief difference in the Agincourt speech from the Harfleur speech is its insistence that the whole English army is a single brotherhood. Before Harfleur Henry addresses each social rank separately, speaking first to 'you noble English', and only eight lines later turning to 'you, good yeomen'. Not until Agincourt does he propose equality. First in a neat pun that puts friendship against fear he offers comradeship:

> We would not die in that man's company
> That fears his fellowship to die with us.
>
> (4.3.38–9)

And then, fellow-feeling assured, he offers the ultimate bond, the blood that will rank the common soldier with his king:

> We few, we happy few, we band of brothers—
> For he today that sheds his blood with me
> Shall be my brother; be he ne'er so vile
> This day shall gentle his condition.
>
> (60–3)

It is a cohesive moment. The noble (commonly identified by a false etymology as the 'non-vile') will be united with the vile in blood. The social divisions emphasised in the Harfleur scenes, where Henry's rallying speech to the separate nobles and yeomen is followed by Llewellyn beating the Eastcheap rogues to the breach and then enjoying a violent quarrel with his fellow-captain MacMorris, distinct marks of a divided army, are now forgotten.

The grandeur of Henry's offer of brotherhood to all his soldiers at Agincourt is given a further context by the insistent acknowledgments of kin in the levels of social ranking that have gone before. In Act 1 brotherhood is exclusively royal or noble. Exeter speaks of Henry's 'brother kings', his ancestors, at 1.2.122. The French king three times calls the threatening Henry 'our brother of England' in 2.4. Henry himself is careful in the early acts to designate his nobles as 'uncle' (Exeter) and 'cousin' (Westmorland, who probably secured his position in the F1 text and was placed at Agincourt by his kinship with Henry, which Henry stresses several times: he is 'cousin' at 1.2.4 and 4.3.19). Henry specifies Gloucester as his 'brother' in 3.7, and at 4.1.3 he greets the arrival who joins him and Gloucester as 'brother Bedford'. After his argument with Bates and Williams, he acknowledges the sound of 'my brother Gloucester's voice', arousing him from prayer before the battle. Only after that does his oration before the battle make every social rank a brother.

—Andrew Gurr, in an introduction to *King Henry V*, by William Shakespeare (Cambridge: Cambridge University Press, 1992), pp. 1–55.

Jonathan Hart on the Play's "Self-Conscious Theatricality"

[Jonathan Hart is author of *Theater and World: The Problematics of Shakespeare's History* and of numerous articles and essays on theory and the Renaissance published in *Textual Practice and Studies in English Literature.* He is a lecturer in the department of English, University of Alberta, Edmonton. In this excerpt, Hart examines the problems of representing history on the stage.]

The Chorus in *Henry V* elaborates self-conscious theatricality in the earlier plays of the tetralogy. He examines the relation of theatre and world, history play and history so much that he raises the audience's awareness of the problems of representing history on the stage. That the main action and the Chorus qualify each other also raises questions about the relation of narrative and represented action in the history play. The Chorus to Act Three asks the audience to 'Suppose,' 'Hear' and 'behold' the men and scenes in his description as actually existing on stage. He challenges the playgoers to do the literally impossible so that they exercise their imaginations as fully as possible. They become part of the meaning of the play and of history. The Chorus realizes the complexity of historical shaping. Repetition becomes a reaching or amplification for the Chorus, who armed with the modest accomplishment of the theatre, at the opening of Act Four, commands the audience to behold, *as may unworthiness define,* Henry among the troops at night, the *disgrace* of *four or five most vile and ragged foils* representing the armies at Agincourt. In addition to this distancing synecdoche, the Chorus also attempts to draw the audience into illusion through the mimetic and onomatopœic descriptions of the busy hammers of the armourers and the French playing for the English at dice. The Chorus to Act Five repeats the view that the play is unable to express actual historical events. The repetition draws attention to itself and stresses the problems of the history play, limiting the genre as being inferior to the world but, at the same time, raising it above the chaos of the world with strong and precise description, ordered couplets and the assumption (from the author's point of view at least) that poetry is more lasting than the memorials of princes. The Chorus also dispels the notion of a monolithic Elizabethan audience, promising to prompt 'those that have not read the story' and asking pardon of those who have because this play is a poor copy of life. Shakespeare displaces a conceit and humility

101

on to his Chorus to this history: this play is more or less than its sources and than the world.

Other aspects of the irony of theatre complicate *Henry V*. Through a character's use of theatrical terms, Shakespeare conveys that character's awareness of 'acting' to an audience watching an actor playing the part. A subsidiary element in this problem play is this self-referential role-playing, so that once again the irony of theatre shows the close relation of *Henry V* to that kind of drama. The other histories, however, also show this characteristic, but this self-conscious sense of theatre supplements in *Henry V* a choric presence that is stronger than anything in the previous plays. For instance, according to Canterbury, the Black Prince *play'd a tragedy* for the French in battle and the Boy says that Nym and Bardolph were much more valorous than Pistol, *this roaring devil i' the old play* (I.ii.105–06; IV.iv.69–74). Most importantly, through the Boy, Shakespeare reminds the audience of morality plays in which the devil is beaten and makes Pistol (not just any old actor) a devil whose vice Fluellen beats out of him with a leek rather than a wooden dagger. Even if the characters refer to role-playing and to early English drama, they cannot understand the application of these references as much as the actors, audience and playwright. This dramatic irony reminds us that this history is dramatic.

Shakespeare's theatrical irony shows that deceit is another disguise, revealing with it the problems of private and public and of government. The history plays especially share this concern with *Measure* and to a lesser extent with *All's Well*. In *Henry V* deceit and disguise test Henry as a ruler (or potential ruler for that matter) more directly and more critically than in *1* and *2 Henry IV*. Shakespeare ensures that the play-goers will appreciate the dramatic irony of the condemnation by Scroop, Cambridge and Grey of a man who insulted the king when, unknown to them, Henry knows that they want to murder him (II.ii). The king is self-consciously theatrical. In order to punish the rebels most and to achieve the greatest effect so that he may appear just when sentencing these men, Henry pretends to reward them with commissions when he hands them a list of their crimes. By way of this dramatic irony, Shakespeare links Henry with the audience and thus appears to seek its approval of the king. Deceit and disguise, such as Pistol's deceit and Henry's disguise, relate closely to each other. The ancient's great voice and seemingly 'gallant service' fool Fluellen until Pistol curses the Welsh captain for not intervening to prevent Bardolph's death and until Gower remembers Pistol as an *arrant counterfeit rascal*. Henry the Fourth had dressed counterfeits in battle to protect his life, so that kings and knaves are not always so different in their theft and deceit. According to the English captain, the ancient will pretend to be a war hero, learning his part, playing the 'roles' of other soldiers and describing the 'scenes' of the battles to be convincing (III.vi.12–82). To compare and contrast this deceit ironically with Henry the Fifth's disguise, the playwright has Henry assume a part among his soldiers before Agincourt and interweaves the incidents of the gloves and the leek.

After encountering Bates and Williams, private soldiers, the king complains about the burden of the public man and the irresponsibility of the private man (IV.i.). This problem of the relation of public and private lies at the heart of kingship from *Richard II* to *Henry V*. With the help of the Boy, Pistol, who did not recognize the disguised king, deceives the French soldier (as Falstaff did to Colevile in 2 *Henry IV*) into thinking him a great warrior. In a soliloquy the Boy exposes Pistol's empty acting to an already suspicious audience (IV.iv.). If Pistol is a hollow man, is Henry? Later, Shakespeare shows Henry 'playing' with Williams as Fluellen does with Pistol, so that playwright once more compares king and Welsh captain and complicates the ironic connections between characters. Henry shares the dramatic irony with the audience at the expense of Williams as well as Fluellen, who is equally ignorant (like Pistol) of the king's earlier disguise and the exchange of gloves and whom Henry asks to be a proxy in a fabricated quarrel with *a friend of Alençon*, which is an actual disagreement with Williams (IV.vii, viii). Shakespeare uses disguise and deceit so extensively that *Henry V* seems to foreshadow *Measure*.

Even though Henry complains about the trials of kingship, he uses his 'directorial' powers, like Duke Vincentio and Prospero, to arrange events and manipulate others. After Henry's good-natured fun is over and Williams and Fluellen have stopped fighting (each having the other's glove), the king rewards Williams, who claims that Henry is at fault for having disguised himself and for not having expected abuse in that guise but who then asks pardon of the king (IV.viii.1–74). It is Henry's power as king that keeps the conflict over the glove from getting out of hand. Whereas the king pretends to be less than he is, Pistol feigns that he is more. The glove gives way to the leek. The hyperbolic and out-of-fashion Fluellen punishes the boasting and antique tongued ancient. Although Pistol likens himself to a horse-leech and is called vicious, on stage he does little to warrant the punishment he receives, except that, if the Boy is to be believed, he is a devil from the old morality plays and must be beaten. In any event, the Welsh captain is less merciful than the king, who, nonetheless, may not have learned as much from Williams as he might have. The taverners continue to raise questions about the nature of kingship and about Henry's dilemmas as king, but they also reveal their own limitations. Henry's tricks as an 'actor' and 'director' show that he is still enraptured by the robes of office even if he sometimes sees the shortcomings of pomp and protocol.

If, most importantly, the irony of theatre in *Henry V* reveals Shakespeare's problematic use of the Chorus, consciously making the audience aware of the limitations and potentialities of the theatre and history play, it also represents other subsidiary elements from the problem plays—theatrical ending, debate and disguise. *Henry V* often uses these aspects in ways that recall their occurrence in *Richard II* and *1* and *2 Henry IV* as well as looking ahead to their use in the problem plays. Although the irony of theatre affirms the close relation of history and the problem play in *Henry V*, it also shows that comparisons that are too close are odious. For instance, the disguised Henry is much like the disguised Duke, but Vincentio is more allegorical and shadowy, more of a god out of the machine than Henry is. On the other hand, Henry must deal with a wider range of public and historical experience and his directorial side (although central to his character) is only one part of a complex character who seems to taste blood, feel desire and laugh more readily than the illusive Duke. Theatrical irony raises our awareness of the problems of the history play and so is a problem play with a difference.

—Jonathan Hart, "Shakespeare's *Henry V:* Towards the Problem Play," in *Cahiers Élisabéthains, Late Medieval and Renaissance English Studies,* no. 42 (October 1992): pp. 20–22.

JONATHAN HART ON THE "PROBLEM OF WORDS" IN THE PLAY

[In this excerpt, Hart continues his discussion of the play's representation of history and the ways in which Shakespeare uses "ironic images of war and peace" to "represent and recreate time."]

Henry's violent images and Burgundy's description of France as a ruined garden most clearly show *Henry V* pressing at the bounds of the genre of the history play, for they reveal a qualification of the comic marriage at the end and modify Henry's heroism. Besides developing aspects of the problem play in *Henry V,* the irony of words complicates such historical patterns as the question of time, much as verbal irony has done in *Richard II* and the *Henry IV* plays. The problem and historical elements overlap.

Ironic images of war and peace best illustrate the problematic attributes of the play. The major speech that modifies Henry's gentleness in war is the threat against Harfleur (III.iii.). Both in love and in war Henry uses violent images. Katherine becomes a sex object and joke about siege and rape (V.ii.309–47). Even the imagery of peace involves strife and ruin as can be observed in Burgundy's image of France as a ruined garden (V.ii.23f.). If this personal violent language spills over into Henry's public conduct of the war and makes his kingship more problematic, references to time also call attention to a crucial question for the history play: how can we best represent and recreate time?

In exploring the problem of representing history in historical drama, we shall concentrate on the views of time expressed by the Chorus and other characters in *Henry V,* although they share many ideas with characters in the first three plays of the tetralogy and although we shall also glance at Henry's Crispin Crispian speech. These shared problems help unite the tetralogy even if the difference in ironic emphasis and in treating problem elements also distinguishes each play. Once again, irony creates a tension between centrifugal and centripetal forces in a history play. In addition to the Chorus' conscious references to history, the views that the characters hold of the past spur them to ironically limited actions. When the Prologue asks the audience to make leaps of imagination, to turn *the accomplishment of many years / Into an hour-glass: for the which supply, / Admit me Chorus to this history,* he offers to act as an intermediary in presenting the history play, especially in making the audience aware of the difference between 'historical' and 'dramatic' time (PR, 30–2). For the Prologue, then, the telescoping of time is important enough to mention at the beginning, suggesting that the representation of this historical period, or, more specifically, a play about this reign demands a radical selection of events and swift representation through narrative foreshortening.

The views of time reflect or refract a divided and fallen world. Shakespeare qualifies the triumph of time that the Chorus proclaims and raises questions about the nature of history. When the Chorus invites the audience to help recreate a specific time, each production creates a novel relation between the eve of Agincourt, the performances of 1599 and their references to Essex, and each new audience (IV, V: CH). The words of the Chorus take on different meanings as time passes. If the playgoers take up the invitation to use their historical imaginations, to participate, they will involve themselves in the interpretation of history (which, with past events and the author's representation, is history) and in the change of history, not as it happened but as people perceive it to have happened. The Chorus talks about other written representations of history and asks the audience, with some irony, to accept the limitations of the theatre in representing historical time (V.CH.1–9). The audience can admire the representation of Agincourt, while realizing that it is not the battle as it happened but an interpretation of it. Playgoers can extrapolate for this limitation the shortcomings of their own interpretations. Paradoxically, Shakespeare's interpretation of the reign of Henry the Fifth is for many the only or primary representation of that period even if it calls attention to its limitations. *Henry V* resembles the Sonnets that are aware of the desolation and constraints of time while defying time with a representation that will survive its human subjects.

Shakespeare modifies the Epilogue's praise of the glory of Henry's 'Small time'. The playwright helps achieve multiplicity by creating a tension between the form, rhythm and musical time of the sonnet that the Epilogue speaks with the ruin he must announce for time ahead. The sonnet is also a coda in a score that not only sings the praises of Henry but also criticizes him. Shakespeare's ironic use of time shows the problems of the genre of the history play, especially in the relation between Chorus and the main action, but, perhaps above all, reveals a common ground between the four plays by representing their shared concerns about human limitations in time.

Nor is history one-sided. For the French, unlike for Henry and Fluellen, Cressy represents the *memorable shame* that Edward inflicted on them at the height of his power and reminds them of Henry, Edward's descendant, who now threatens France (II.iv.53–64). Although the French king states a particular lesson of history—that the Dauphin should learn to respect the English—he later does not follow it himself and rejects Henry's 'memorable' pedigree that would give him the French crown (II.iv.88). Memory also fails the characters. It takes Gower a while to remember that Pistol is *a bawd, a cut-purse* (III.vi.61–62). Here, Shakespeare causes an "unhistorical" character to judge another like him as if to complicate history through the supposition of how things might have been. To inspire his own soldiers in the Crispin Crispian speech, Henry reminds them that although as old men they will forget other events, they will remember this great day, each man recalling his own feats with exaggeration, passing on the story of English honour to his son, who will teach his son, so that Crispin Crispian will never be forgotten until the *ending of the world* (IV.iii.40–66). Henry shows a subtle understanding of subjectivity, embellishment and myth-making, of the difficulty of keeping history from becoming an epic or romantic narrative, and of the advantages to his situation and to heroism that the difficulty allows. Oral history is important to Henry for reasons of self-interest, patriotism and heroism even as he understands its departure from fact and truth. For Henry, as for many of us, the truth is never plain and rarely simple. The truth of fiction and the fiction of truth interact to the very end of the tetralogy. Irony of words helps reveal the problem play in *Henry V,* which presses at the bounds of its genre, including from more problematic 'images' such as those of war and peace as well as more commonly historic ones like 'time.'

—Jonathan Hart, "Shakespeare's Henry V: Towards the Problem Play," in *Cahiers Élisabéthains, Late Medieval and Renaissance English Studies,* no. 42 (October 1992): pp. 27–28.

P. K. AYERS ON HARRY AS "CHAMELEON LINGUIST"

[P. K. Ayers teaches Renaissance literature at Memorial University of Newfoundland. His works include the study of shifting patterns of language usage in late sixteenth- and early seventeenth-century British drama. In this excerpt, Ayers examines the way in which, through his linguistic genius, "the Hal, Harry, or Henry on display is the one those around him want or need to see."]

Henry's scene with Catherine resonates with echoes of the past, most notably those of another plain-spoken soldier named Harry and his Kate. The contrast they provide is illuminating. In his scenes with Lady

Percy, Hotspur demonstrates a simplicity of speech that does exactly what Henry is claiming to do but does not. Within the context of his linguistic playfulness, words and meanings are clearly linked; saying what he means and meaning what he says, in other words, Hotspur uses rhetorical performance to reveal rather than conceal himself.

Hotspur's speech demonstrates his more general appeal to our sympathies, despite his obvious and appalling limitations of character. Certainly the portrait of domestic felicity that it generates is not easily matched in its warmth and tenderness elsewhere in Shakespeare; to it Lady Percy's profoundly moving elegy in *2 Henry IV* offers its own kind of testimonial. It is an appeal that stands in some contrast to the disquiet inevitably produced in Henry's case by what is manifestly a performance, however skillful, of speech that depends for its effect upon its sincerity. Hotspur's version by contrast establishes a claim to truth that Henry's cannot. It acquires the kind of moral significance, the larger linguistic and ethical integrity, that is traditionally associated with plain speech. Henry, using the same style, instead subverts the expectations it arouses.

Henry's appropriation of Hotspur's distinctive style at the climax of his own career is only the final example in a much longer and more complex sequence of such borrowings. In *1 Henry IV*, Hal, reducing Hotspur to his factor, promises his father in appropriately mercantile terms to appropriate the stock of glory that Hotspur has acquired on his behalf. By covering Hotspur's face with his "favours," Hal suggests another kind of assumption of his role. At the end of *2 Henry IV* it is his name at stake, with all the implications that attach themselves to it, as Henry reassures his followers after the death of his father:

> This is the English not the Turkish court;
> Not Amurath an Amurath succeeds,
> But Harry Harry.
>
> (V.ii.47–49)

It is a sequence in which, as Richard Hillman has noted, Hotspur becomes the unstated middle term.

The issue of names and identities is further complicated by the fact that Henry is here not so much identifying as renaming, and thus recreating, himself. Having been linked as "Harry" to Hotspur from the beginning of *1 Henry IV*, he formally rejects the appellation when challenged by his rival. He now reassumes it, but simultaneously, as Falstaff so shortly discovers, rejects the identity apparently attached to it, namely that of his younger self; the succession is in this sense less that of father to son than that of the old self to the new one about to be celebrated in the final moments of *2 Henry IV*. During this process he assumes the identity most closely associated with the name, in effect turning Hotspur into both his progenitor and *alter ego*.

In the doubling of the two Harrys, it is not without interest, *pace* Dr. Johnson, that the prince's first reference to the other Harry focuses on the precise linguistic issues raised by his own wooing of his Catherine. He ridicules, that is, Hotspur's version of the plain style through the dismissive comparison of his linguistic habits to those of Francis the drawer, and beyond him the parrot to which both are ultimately compared:

> That ever this fellow should have fewer words than a
> parrot, and yet the son of a woman! His industry is
> upstairs and downstairs, his eloquence the parcel of a reck-
> oning. I am not yet of Percy's mind, the Hotspur of the
> North—he that kills me some six or seven dozen of Scots
> at a breakfast, washes his hands and says to his wife, "Fie
> upon this quiet life! I want work." "O my sweet Harry,"
> says she, "how many hast thou killed today?" "Give my
> roan horse a drench," says he, and answers, "Some four-
> teen," an hour after; "a trifle, a trifle."
>
> (II.v.99–109)

The brilliance of the parody is given dramatic emphasis by its position directly after the first scene in question, where Kate is indeed displaced by a crop-eared roan. The larger charge, moreover, is clearly a serious one. Parrots offer a mocking parody of the defining characteristic of humankind, which is indeed to be able to define itself through the gift of rational speech. Words are the basic units of the linguistic microcosm that extends to the macrocosmic *Logos;* to be without them, like Francis, is to be without essential humanity.

Hotspur's deficiencies of language, beyond Lady Percy's ambiguous reference to his "thickness of speech," are obvious enough. His plainess is often simple rudeness, displayed most frequently to all whose linguistic mannerisms differ from his own. His attack on the foppish lord who demanded the prisoners focuses in large part upon the "holiday and lady terms" (I.iii.45) in which the demand is made; likewise he mocks Kate for swearing "like a comfit-maker's wife" rather than with "a good mouth-filling oath" (III.i.246–50).

The connection with parrots, moreover, is not without foundation. In his planned revenge on the king, Hotspur imagines a starling that will be a substitute for himself (I.iii.219–23), and is later called, affectionately but appropriately, a paraquito by Lady Percy (II.iv.83). All too often he indulges in a solipsistic mode of compulsively noncommunicative speech that excludes all other speakers. Thus Worcester complains that Hotspur will "lend no ear unto my purposes" (I.iii.216), while Northumberland more sharply rebukes him for "Tying thine ear to no tongue but thine own" (I.iii.236).

Yet for all the brilliance of the parody and the seriousness of Hotspur's limitations, Hal is clearly wrong. Hotspur is in most respects an impressive speaker. His range is wide, encompassing that playfully domestic banter with Kate, the epic account of Mortimer's fight, the flights of poetic fancy in his visionary dreams of glory, the public declamations of a war leader, and the philosophic intensity of his dying words. His linguistic self-consciousness is as acute as Hal's, as the parallel word-play on "calling" with Glendower and Francis seems designed to establish.

What is most striking about Hotspur's use of language, however, is neither its range nor sophistication, but the sense it conveys of the speaker himself. In whatever style he uses, his voice is unmistakable, and the *persona* remains constant. However wide his range, Hotspur remains univocal, using language in all the various contexts of *1 Henry IV* to define himself in consistent terms. His contempt for the "certain lord" and his rebuke of Kate both spring from their failures to do likewise. Plain speech for Hotspur simply provides the clearest illustration of the simplicity that defines his more general linguistic practice; like Hal, Hotspur claims to "have not well the gift of tongue" (V.ii.77), but here the *topos* is used without obvious irony.

The contrast initiated by Hal, however, is instructive. In range Hal is clearly Hotspur's superior, but it is precisely this range that is the source of the difficulties associated with his role. Unlike Hotspur, he tends to acquire the voices of those whose language he is speaking, to end up sounding like them. It is indeed for so doing that he is most frequently praised by them. Not only is he multilingual, he is polyvocal. With the king, that is, he sounds rather like the king himself, brisk and to the point; with Falstaff he sounds like Falstaff, intoxicated with his own wit; with Francis he sounds like Francis, prosaic and senseless. Hal disappears into his roles; indeed it would seem to be his need to become Francis at least temporarily that lies behind the disturbing oddity of the tavern scene, namely the brutality with which the harmless and well-meaning drawer is mocked.

Harry's genius here in a sense becomes his curse; the chameleon linguist reflects in his speech not himself, but the expectations of those to whom he speaks. He himself becomes in the process largely invisible; the Hal, Harry, or Henry on display is the one those around him want or need to see. Such invisibility exacts its own price, however, as the would-be observer, frustrated in the search for a palpable core of "identity" or "character" through the traditional analysis of speech acts, is obliged to create whatever kind of protagonist seems most appropriate to the circumstances. The result is the cacophony of critical voices that surrounds the figure of Henry in all his guises.

—P. K. Ayers, "'Fellows of Infinite Tongue': Henry V and the King's English," in *Studies in English Literature 1500–1900* 34, no. 2 (Spring 1994): pp. 255–258.

[In this excerpt, Bloom remarks upon the irony of Henry's "mastery of power" against the loss of Falstaff and an "education in wit."]

This brilliant and subtle work will always be popular; I could say "for the wrong reasons," except that all reasons for Shakespeare's eternal popularity are correct, one way or another. And yet *Henry V* is clearly a lesser drama than the two parts of *Henry IV*. Falstaff is gone, and King Henry V, matured into the mastery of power, is less interesting than the ambivalent Prince Hal, whose potential was more varied. The great Irish poet W. B. Yeats made the classic comment on this aesthetic falling away in his *Ideas of Good and Evil:*

> [Henry V] has the gross vices, the coarse nerves, of one who is to rule among violent people, and he is so little "too friendly" to his friends that he bundles them out of door when their time is over. He is as remorseless and undistinguished as some natural force, and the finest thing in his play is the way his old companions fall out of it brokenhearted or on their way to the gallows.

I read the play that Yeats read, but much Shakespeare scholarship reads otherwise. *Henry V* is now most widely known because of the films quarried from it by Laurence Olivier and Kenneth Branagh. Both movies are lively, patriotic romps, replete with exuberant bombast, provided by Shakespeare himself, with what degree of irony we cannot quite tell but are free to surmise:

> We few, we happy few, we band of brothers;
> For he to-day that sheds his blood with me
> Shall be my brother; be he ne'er so vile
> This day shall gentle his condition:
> And gentlemen in England, now a-bed,
> Shall think themselves accurs'd they were not here,
> And hold their manhoods cheap whiles any speaks
> That fought with us upon Saint Crispin's day.
> [IV.iii.60–67]

That is the King, just before the battle of Agincourt. He is very stirred; so are we; but neither we nor he believes a word he says. The common soldiers fighting with their monarch are not going to become gentlemen, let alone nobles, and "the ending of the world" is a rather grand evocation for an imperialist land grab that did not long survive Henry V's death, as Shakespeare's audience knew too well. Hazlitt, with characteristic eloquence, joins Yeats as the true exegete of Henry V and his play:

He was a hero, that is, he was ready to sacrifice his own life for the pleasure of destroying thousands of other lives. . . . How then do we like him? We like him in the play. There he is a very amiable monster, a very splendid pageant. . . .

This cannot be bettered, but is that all Prince Hal matured into: an amiable monster, a splendid pageant? Yes; for this, Falstaff was rejected, Bardolph was hanged, and a great education in wit was partly thrown away. Shakespeare's ironic insight remains highly relevant; power keeps its habit through the ages. Our nation's Henry V (some might say) was John Fitzgerald Kennedy, who gave us the Bay of Pigs and the enhancement of our Vietnam adventure. Some scholars may moralize and historicize until they are purple with pride, but they will not persuade us that Shakespeare (playwright *and* man) preferred his amiable monster to the genius of Falstaff, and his splendid pageant to the varied and vital *Henry IV* plays.

—Harold Bloom, *Shakespeare, The Invention of the Human* (New York: Riverhead Books, 1998), pp. 319–320.

Works by William Shakespeare

Venus and Adonis. 1593.

The Rape of Lucrece. 1594.

Henry VI. 1594.

Titus Andronicus. 1594.

The Taming of the Shrew. 1594.

Romeo and Juliet. 1597.

Richard III. 1597.

Richard II. 1597.

Love's Labour's Lost. 1598.

Henry IV. 1598.

The Passionate Pilgrim. 1599.

A Midsummer Night's Dream. 1600.

The Merchant of Venice. 1600.

Much Ado About Nothing. 1600.

Henry V. 1600.

The Phoenix and the Turtle. 1601.

The Merry Wives of Windsor. 1602.

Hamlet. 1603.

King Lear. 1608.

Troilus and Cressida. 1609.

Sonnets. 1609.

Pericles. 1609.

Othello. 1622.

Mr. William Shakespeares Comedies, Histories & Tragedies. Ed. John Heminge and Henry Condell. 1623 (First Folio), 1632 (Second Folio), 1663 (Third Folio), 1685 (Fourth Folio).

Poems. 1640.

Works. Ed. Nicholas Rowe. 1709. 6 vols.

Works. Ed. Alexander Pope. 1723–25. 6 vols.

Works. Ed. Lewis Theobald. 1733. 7 vols.

Works. Ed. Thomas Hanmer. 1743–44. 6 vols.

Works. Ed. William Warburton. 1747. 8 vols.

Plays. Ed. Samuel Johnson. 1765. 8 vols.

Plays and Poems. Ed. Edmond Malone. 1790. 10 vols.

The Family Shakespeare. Ed. Thomas Bowdler. 1807. 4 vols.

Works. Ed. J. Payne Collier. 1842–44. 8 vols.

Works. Ed. H. N. Hudson. 1851–56. 11 vols.

Works. Ed. Alexander Dyce. 1857. 6 vols.

Works. Ed. Richard Grant White. 1857–66. 12 vols.

Works (Cambridge Edition). Ed. William George Clark, John Glover, and William Aldis Wright. 1863–66. 9 vols.

A New Variorum Edition of the Works of Shakespeare. Ed. H. H. Furness et al. 1871–   .

Works. Ed. W. J. Rolfe. 1871–96. 40 vols.

The Pitt Press Shakespeare. Ed. A. W. Verity. 1890–1905. 13 vols.

The Warwick Shakespeare. 1893–1938. 13 vols.

The Temple Shakespeare. Ed. Israel Gollancz. 1894–97. 40 vols.

The Arden Shakespeare. Ed W. J. Craig, R. H. Case et al. 1899–1924. 37 vols.

The Shakespeare Apocrypha. Ed. C. F. Tucker Brooke. 1908.

The Yale Shakespeare. Ed. Wilbur L. Cross, Tucker Brooke, and Willard Highley Durham. 1912–27. 40 vols.

The New Shakespeare (Cambridge Edition). Ed. Arthur Quiller-Couch and John Dover Wilson. 1921–62. 38 vols.

The New Temple Shakespeare. Ed. M. R. Ridley. 1934–36. 39 vols.

Works. Ed. George Lyman Kittredge. 1936.

The Penguin Shakespeare. Ed. G. B. Harrison. 1937–59. 36 vols.

The New Clarendon Shakespeare. Ed. R. E. C. Houghton. 1938–   .

The Arden Shakespeare. Ed. Una Ellis-Fermor et al. 1951–   .

The Complete Pelican Shakespeare. Ed. Alfred Harbage. 1969.

The Complete Signet Classic Shakespeare. Ed. Sylvan Barnet. 1972.

The Oxford Shakespeare. Ed. Stanley Wells. 1982–   .

The New Cambridge Shakespeare. Ed. Philip Brockbank. 1984–   .

Works about
William Shakespeare's Histories

Baker, David J. *Between Nations: Shakespeare, Spenser, Marvell, and the Question of Britain.* Stanford, Calif.: Stanford University Press, 1997.

Becker, George J. *Shakespeare's Histories.* Ungar, 1977.

Bergeron, David M., ed. *Pageantry in the Shakespearean Theater.* Athens, Ga.: University of Georgia Press, 1986.

Blanpied, John. *Time and the Artist in Shakespeare's History Plays.* Newark, Del.: University of Delaware Press, 1983.

Bloom, Harold. *Shakespeare: The Invention of the Human.* New York: Riverhead Books, 1998.

————, ed. *William Shakespeare's Henry IV, Part 1.* New York: Chelsea House, 1987.

————, ed. *Falstaff.* New York: Chelsea House, 1992.

Bradley, A. C. *Shakespearean Tragedy.* London: The Macmillian Co., 1904.

Calderwood, James. *Metadrama in Shakespeare's* Henriad. Berkeley, Calif.: University of California Press, 1979.

Everett, Barbara. "The Fatness of Falstaff: Shakespeare and Character." *Proceedings of the British Academy* 76 (1990): 109–28.

Gash, Anthony. "Shakespeare's Comedies of Shadow and Substance: Word and Image in *Henry IV* and *Twelfth Night.*" *Word and Image* 4 (1988): 626–62.

Holderness, Graham. *Shakespeare's Histories.* New York: St. Martin, 1985.

Howard, Jean E. *Engendering a Nation: A Feminist Account of Shakespeare's English Histories.* New York: Routledge, 1997.

Jones, Robert C. *These Valiant Dead: Renewing the Past in Shakespeare's Histories.* Iowa City, Iowa: University of Iowa Press, 1991.

Levine, Nina S. *Women's Matters: Politics, Gender, and Nation in Shakespeare's Early History Plays.* Newark, Del.: University of Delaware Press, 1998.

Manheim, Michael. *The Weak King Dilemma in the Shakespearean History Play.* Syracuse, N.Y.: Syracuse University Press, 1973.

Meron, Theodore. *Bloody Constraint: War and Chivalry in Shakespeare.* New York: Oxford, 1998.

Pierce, Robert B. *Shakespeare's History Plays: The Family and the State.* Columbus: Ohio State University Press, 1971.

Prior, Moody E. *The Drama of Power: Studies in Shakespeare's History Plays.* Evanston, Ill.: Northwestern University Press, 1973.

Racklin, Phyllis. *Stages of History: Shakespeare's English Chronicles.* Ithaca, N.Y.: Cornell University Press, 1990.

Ribner, Irving. *The English History Play in the Age of Shakespeare.* Princeton, N.J.: Princeton University Press, 1957.

Smidt, Kristian. *Unconformities in Shakespeare's History Plays.* London: Macmillan, 1982.

Thayer, C. G. *Shakespearean Politics: Government and Misgovernment in the Great Histories.* Athens: Ohio University Press, 1983.

Tillyard, E. M. W. *Shakespeare's History Plays.* London: Chatto & Windus, 1944.

Watson, Donald G. *Shakespeare's Early History Plays: Politics at Play on the Elizabethan Stage.* Athens, Ga.: University of Georgia Press, 1990.

Wilson, J. Dover. *The Essential Shakespeare.* New York: Cambridge University Press, 1932.

Index of
Themes and Ideas

Westmoreland in, 58, 61, 70; Worcester in, 35, 36, 37, 38, 48, 49, 50, 108; Archbishop of York in, 51, 58, 59, 61, 68